STRONG LAD WANTED FOR STRONG LASS

Growing Up in Carlisle

Hunter Davies

Bookcase

First published 2004
Copyright Hunter Davies 2004
Published by Bookcase, 17-19 Castle Street, Carlisle. CA3 8SY
ISBN 190414705 4

Introduction

I love Carlisle. Every day in every way, it seems to become better, cleaner, prettier, with more attractions, more facilities, more life. It even seems to grow more ancient, more historic, which can't quite be true. History doesn't get acquired overnight, not something you send away for in the post or on the net. It must always have been there, just lurking in the background. Like so much of Carlisle life.

People today often chance upon it, tourists and visitors with little preconceived knowledge, having had only a rough idea of where it was, often confusing it in their minds with some place else, perhaps in Scotland or even Wales, then they go away raving about the Old Town Hall, the Castle, the Cathedral, Abbey Street and Castle Street, the Old Covered Market or the sparkling new Lanes, as if they have discovered a hidden gem. Which in a way they have.

Carlisle was my home town until the age of 22, yet through all those years, so much of it was hidden from me, or perhaps, as I've come to believe, hidden from itself, disguised as some other place, cloaked in the wrong raiment.

I might be extolling its virtues now, but my memories of Carlisle in the 1950's was of a dirty, dreary, noisy, smoky, industrial town. That's firstly what I see when I look back in my mind. There seemed

3

to be factories everywhere, belching smoke, surrounded by grime. I can see no trees or green places in the middle of the town when I look back, no flowers, no pretty bits. The Castle was there, had been there since 1092, but cut off by narrow, decaying slum streets. Botchergate and London Road was frightening, with huge cranes and monster machineries lumbering in and out of Cowans Sheldon. Dixon's chimney and its factory was overwhelming, towering above the city, ready to trample over all humans. Going to the public baths in James Street, you risked being swallowed up or choked to death by the fumes and dust from the Metal Box factory. Denton Holme seemed to be just one big works, all human life revolving round Ferguson's or Prachitts. Caldewgate, dominated by Carr's biscuits works, was the scariest place of all, full of toughs and the deprived, who would beat you up if you looked at them.

You had to time it carefully, going Up Street, listening for the hooters and horns, else you might be swept along or knocked over by the human tide which engulfed all local streets when a shift finished and out streamed thousands of workers from Carr's, Cowan's, Fergusons', Stead McAlpine, Morton Sundour, Hudson Scott (which Metal Box was still known by) or the Brewery.

Being a Carr's cracker packer was what girls ended up doing, if nothing else presented itself, or for a boy, it was working as a cleaner on the railway. Yet when I look now at my collection of Carr's memorabilia, a lot of it from the 1950's, admire the images and art work on their boxes, the booklets showing photographs of immaculate, cheerful women workers on the production lines, I must have seen all this, at the time, but I never thought of it as in any way romantic or attractive. This image is fostered further if you visit Tullie House Museum today and see the pretty railway carriages, the colourful livery of the old railway companies which onced streamed in and out of Carlisle's Citadel Station. I was there, at the time, when the old steam engines were still running, but I don't remember any colours or prettiness or romance, just smoke and noise and dust, clutching my throat whenever I stepped into the Citadel Station.

Is my memory at fault? Perhaps marginally. There must be people who at the time thought Carlisle was a nice and pretty place, because they remembered when it was much worse, during the depression and unemployment of the 1930's.

Factually, there is little argument. The 1951 census shows that well over half of all Carlisle's workers over the age of 15, some 11,000 of them, worked in what we would now call heavy duty, blue collar manufacturing - such as engineering, textiles, railways and transport. Only 4,500 had white collar jobs, most of them being clerks. In 1958, 61% of Carlisle's population lived in council houses, as I did, the total being 9,638. Today, only 15% of Carlisle people live in council property, the rest either owning or renting private property.

Carlisle has now radically changed, most of the old belching factories gone, the majority of workers are of the white collar type, sitting in offices, and the city has been cleaned up.

In the 1950's, I probably never gave a second glance to the Old Town Hall, unaware that it was a classic 17th century building, that underneath there was some pretty pink stone, longing to be revealed. Partly because of all the exterior grime, but mainly because I was too busy trying to fight my way through the awful traffic to get on the C3 Ribble bus to St Ann's Hill. The area round the Town Hall, now lovingly cobbled, a flower bedecked pedestrianised open space, was in effect one big bus stop, the main departure and arrival point for all

5

the city buses. It was as busy and manic as Piccadilly Circus, even worse at the time of the Glasgow Fair when the whole of the city came to a standstill. Before the coming of the ring road and the M6, the centre of Carlisle was literally the main road between England and Scotland. Few ordinary families had their own cars, yet in Lowther Street in 1958, there were 1,500 vehicles per hour in the rush hour. During the Glasgow Fair, traffic jams could stretch for about five miles, from Carleton, London Road, Botchergate, Lowther Street, through Stanwix and Scotland Road, practically all the way to Gretna.

Take off your specs, my dear, let your hair flow free, give up those dowdy clothes, has anyone told you what a nice complexion you have? You do look lovely when you smile. Why, you could be quite pretty. So why not try it, my dear.

And that's what happened to Carlisle. It had a face lift, an image make-over, revealing nice things we either had not seen, or did not know were there because they had become obscured, sullied and spoiled.

I have to admit that when I lived in Carlisle, my ambition in life was not to live in Carlisle. I wanted to get away, leave it all behind. Carlisle the place seemed to depress and oppress me, crowd in on me, was always grey and overcast.

It wasn't of course just the fabric and physical look of the city. It was me as well - teenagers feel frustrated, want to escape, be anywhere but where they are. I would probably have felt much the same in Bath or Brighton, places which to most English minds have always appeared desirable and attractive, at least to people not living there. Carlisle has never had that image. Until now.

As Carlisle has changed, so have I. Not just in now loving the City, but with age, as I look back, I can see that whatever I might have thought at the time, it was the source of so many of the most important influences in my life and yes, where exciting things did happen to me . . .

Chapter One

Crossing The Border

I boast I am from Carlisle, go on about it being my home town, but I'm a foreigner, really, which is what I felt like for many years. Perhaps that's one reason why it seemed so frightening and ugly and why it took me so long to discover its charms.

I was born on January 7, 1936, at Thornhill maternity hospital in Johnstone, Renfrewshire. So it says on my birth certificate, but I have no memory of Johnstone and have never been back since. I wouldn't recognize Johnstone if I met it in my porridge. That's one of the phrases my mother used, which I picked up, and which now my London born children use, to the bemusement of their friends.

My earliest memory is of being pushed in my pram through crowds and mud to see the launch of the Queen Mary at John Brown's shipyard on the Clyde. What a great day that was, a proud event for millions of Scottish people as Scottish built ships were famous throughout the world, so every Scot believed. The Queen Mary was in fact launched in 1934, so some confusion there. Could

Above: My father and mother with me in the middle aged four, and twin sisters Annabelle and Marion in Deer Park Road, Carlisle, 1940.

it have been the Queen Elizabeth which was launched in 1938? Possibly. This memory of going to a launch could well be a received memory. I was only told about it later by my mother. It was probably the launch of some minor ship, but I adopted it, convincing myself I was there on a great national occasion.

Both my parents were Scottish. My mother, Marion Brechin, came from Motherwell and my father, John Hunter Davies, from Cambuslang. My mother's parents lived in a council house on the Bellshill Road in Motherwell and I spent many holidays with them. I didn't like their house, an upstairs flat really, and my grandfather never spoke. He just sat, silently whistling, a constant hissing noise that never turned into a tune while he unravelled knots in balls of string, smiling to himself. Now and again, he did play Ludo with me. My grandmother Brechin was small and fierce, always fussing about my vest, making me wash my hands whenever I sat down to look at the photographs in her big, glittery book about the Royal Family which she'd got through the Daily Express.

Opposite their house was The Bing - an overgrown spoil heap from a disused coal mine - on which I played with the Wallace boys from the Buildings further down the Bellshill Road. These were older tenement blocks, with brutal outside concrete landings and communal washhouses in the backyard. I preferred the Buildings to my grandmother's flat because they were always full of children running about, skipping, playing football, with mothers shouting from the landings for them.

My grandfather Brechin had been on the railways, ending up as an engine driver, which my mother told me was a very good job, people were proud of it, especially as it gave you free travel. They hardly travelled anywhere, so it didn't seem much of an advantage. And if his job had been so good, why were they living in a pokey, very cold, one bedroom council flat.

My Davies grandparents, over in Cambuslang, seemed much posher, higher class. They owned their own house on the Hamilton Road with a garden. They had books in the house and an attic room and a hole-in-the-wall bed in the main living room. This was just an alcove, filled by a double bed, hidden behind a screen, typical of

My mother Marion and father John in their early married years in the 1930's

many Scottish homes of the time. They also had a clothes pulley suspended from the ceiling in the living room which I loved pulling up and down.

My father's sister Jean had been to Hamilton Academy and Glasgow University, and had become a teacher. His brother Alex was also a teacher. Another brother Jim, despite working as a rent collector and various other jobs, was really a poet and playwright, so I was led to believe. He did have a play produced at the Byre Theatre in St Andrews which everyone in the family went to see. It was a biblical play, called The Hands of Esau, written in the Scots dialect. When I got a bit older, he insisted on reading it out to me. It seemed to go on for hours. I couldn't understand a word and eventually I fell asleep which rather hurt him.

Grandfather Davies had been some sort of engineer, probably little more than a fitter, upper working class, not professional class, but the Scottish education system had always been better, more enlightened, more open to all classes than in England and so several of his children had received higher education in the 1930's and done quite well for themselves. Except for my Dad, who had left school at 14. But unlike my Motherwell relatives, who were blue collar workers, he became a white collar worker, a clerk attached to the Air Force.

At the time of my birth, he was still serving in the RAF. I have several photos of him in uniform, one of them with the Duke of Hamilton sitting in the front row, so he told me, who was his commanding officer, and also snaps of him in an RAF football team.

It was through the RAF he met my mother Marion. She also had left school at fourteen and became a maid, serving in the house of a Baptist minister. One of the guests when she was there, to whom she had to bring tea in bed, was the Rev Eric Liddell, formerly a well known Scottish runner whose life was portrayed in Chariots of Fire. She then got a job as a waitress in the NAAFI in Perth where my father happened to be stationed. I always sensed my father's family rather looked down on my mother socially. She certainly felt inferior to the teachers in his family, especially his sister Jean, who seemed to my mother to be so clever, so organised, having a career and running

My father in the RAF, back row, third from left, early 1930's

11

Studio snap of me, right, plus sisters Marion and Annabelle

a family with her house always immaculate. My mother, overburdened by so many things could never be said to have run an immaculate house.

While we were still living in Johnstone, with my father still in the RAF, my mother had twins, Marion and Annabelle, who were born in 1939. My father was carried shoulder high round the station, as if it had been a triumph for him personally. Not long afterwards, in 1940, we moved to Carlisle where my younger brother Johnny was born in 1941. My father had been posted to 14 MU in Carlisle, an RAF maintenance unit. By this time he was a civilian, but working with the RAF as a wages clerk.

One of my earliest Carlisle memories is of going with him in some sort of RAF jeep, guarded by two uniformed RAF men, while we travelled round some RAF stations, taking the wages. I thought it was very exciting, the first time I had ever been in any sort of motor vehicle. We stopped somewhere, possibly a pub, while the RAF types listened to the Grand National on a radio. We never had a car in our family, nor surprisingly did any of my Cambuslang relatives, though we always looked upon them as rich.

In Carlisle we lived at 25 Deer Park Road on the St Ann's Hill estate. It was a recently built 1930's council estate, and rent was collected by the council every week. The fathers of almost all my friends worked at the nearby 14 MU which had been established in 1938 before the RAF took over the old Kingstown Aerodrome. Thousands of people worked there at the time, spread over several sites to the North of the City. It supplied the whole of the RAF with various sorts of parts, hence all the hangars, warehouses and men who called themselves storemen.

There were apparently seven such depots spread around the UK, all classified as secret, and each of them held a complete range of stock, in case any of them got hit by an air attack. At the height of the war, in 1945, there were 4,300 people employed at Carlisle's 14MU - 784 uniformed airmen and the rest civilians. A good half of the civilian workers were women, who were replaced by men in the post-war years. It's only now when I have looked up details of 14MU in Carlisle's reference library, that I have realised what an enormous enterprise it was. A town on its own, with its own life and legends. There was, for example, 13 miles of railtrack on the site.

I assume our part of the estate had been built to serve 14 MU, or that's what it became, for the MU was the focal point of our lives. As children we would go to sports

25 Deer Park Road today.

days and similar events held at 14 MU. During the War, it was well guarded, seemed very hush hush and important, as if real war work was being done there. I was not aware of any bombs falling on Carlisle during the war, but we could hear the German bombers flying overhead, on their way to Glasgow or Belfast. There was a rumour once that a Jerry plane had come down at Kingstown and I went with some other boys to look for it in Kingmoor Woods, but never found it.

After the war, by the time of the 1950's, 14 MU became a bit of a joke in Carlisle, a soft option, full of pen pushers and blokes wandering around in overalls who seemed to have little work to do.

But it carried on for several more decades, providing supply support in 1982 for the Falklands War and the Gulf War of 1990. It finally closed in 1994 by which time it was down to 734 permanent staff who were still, valiantly, managing to keep track and stock of some 58 million once-vitally-important individual items. I think my dad, when he was there, had something to do with note pads or perhaps paper clips. I know we always had a lot in the house.

Next door to us in Deer Park Road we had a cockney woman, Mrs Jarret and her family. Several people in the street took in evacuees, but we never had any, as far as I can remember, probably because we were now a family of six in a small council house.

My best friend was Reggie Hill, who lived in the next street to us in Fraser Grove. Beyond that was Hallaway. Behind us was Hartley Avenue. Running down the end of our road was Caird Avenue. I was told, some time later, while still living in Carlisle, that these streets were all named after well known doctors who practised in Carlisle in the 1930's - presumably Doctors Fraser, Caird, Hartley and Hallaway. I was then told that the Dr Fraser in question was the father of George MacDonald Fraser, the author of Flashman, one of Carlisle Grammar School's best known sons. This idea has always delighted me and I've repeated it, as a fact.

Having finished this book, I thought I had better settle this question once and for all, if I'm going to put it in writing, so I wrote to George MacDonald Fraser in the Isle of Man, where he lives, to ask him if it was true. This was his interesting reply:

14

Dear Hunter Davies,

There were four Dr Frasers in Carlisle before the war: my father ("Doctor Willy"), my uncle (Doctor Allan"), and two who were no relation, Kenneth and Mark. Kenneth was Medical Officer, and I think Fraser Grove was named after him -- but it might have been after Mark, whose wife was very big in women's organisations in the town.

Altogether there have been eleven Dr Frasers in Carlisle. I should have been a twelfth, but wasn't, thank heaven.

Odd that your letter, referring to Old Carliols, should arrive on the one day for many years that I wore my Old Carliol tie. The occasion was a lunch at which my wife Kathy (formerly Hetherington) met an old classmate from the High School. We all agreed that Carlisle is not what it was.

All the best,

Yours aye,

Reggie Hill, my friend who lived in Fraser Grove, was known as Toddles. Even at the age of five and six, he didn't like his mother or his family calling him Toddles. I presume it started because as a toddler he toddled along. I would call him Toddles, just to annoy, but

Stanwix Primary School today

not for very long as he soon grew much taller than me and could therefore beat me up.

We both started at the same time at Stanwix Primary School about a mile away in what is still today seen as one of the posher parts of Carlisle. At the time, and for many years, it was the nearest primary school to our estate, so we had to go there, but we always felt a social divide, that the ones who actually lived in Stanwix were the elite who lived in houses owned by their parents with their own door-bell and a garage, sometimes even a car to go in it, while we were the council house scruffs. As some of the teachers made quite clear.

I suppose my mother must have taken me to Stanwix School in the early weeks when I first started, but I was soon going on the bus myself, along with Reggie and the other kids from the St Ann's Hill estate. No one would let kids of five or six go on buses on their own today, or even walk to school unattended, but it was normal at the time, what everyone did. Me and Reg and another friend from the next street, Georgie Ratcliffe, would be out for hours, raking round the estate, mucking around in the allotments behind Caird Avenue, going into the new council houses being built at Briar Bank and climbing on the scaffolding, playing endless games on our own in Kingmoor Woods or in the surrounding fields, building dams, paddling in streams. All memoirists of the 1940's and 1950's have such rosy images of unattended childhood play, but we did, we did.

One day, when I was about seven, Reg and I were waiting at the top of Stanwix for the Ribble bus to take us home after school. We let several buses pass us because we wanted to come home on the Dummy, which was a smaller bus, a funny shaped bus, as if it had been cut in half. It was just another Ribble bus, the same price, for the public at large, not confined to school children. We just liked it better.

We got on, with a gang of other kids, who also liked this bus, so naturally there was a lot of pushing and shoving as we all tried to get to the back. Being at the back of the bus, up against the back door, was the place to be. As the bus was going down Etterby Street, which is a steep cobbled hill, leading down from Stanwix towards St Ann's, it always got up a good speed, rattling over the cobbles, which added to the excitement of being on the Dummy. The emergency door with a big handle at the back of the bus was not to be opened or even touched by anyone, but suddenly it flew open. Some kids had probably been tampering with it, or perhaps Reg and I had touched it. I don't think it was the fault of the Ribble bus company. But the result was that Reg and I fell out together - right into the path of a lorry which was following behind the bus.

Somehow, the lorry managed to avoid us, not that we were aware of it swerving or braking to stop itself running over us. That was what we were subsequently told. The fall from the bus, probably going at 40 miles an hour, had rendered us both immediately unconscious. I knew nothing about anything until I woke up in hospital. It was only many years later, when I grew up, supposedly, did I ever wonder what our respective mothers must have been put through. Neither of us had a phone or a car. It was the arrival of a policeman at each of our houses which informed our mothers that there had been a road accident and that we were both lying in the Carlisle Infirmary. They then had to catch a bus to town, to find out how we were.

I don't know how long I was in there, or what the injuries were, but we knew we had had a very lucky escape What a loss to literature that would have been for Toddles is now Reginald C Hill, one of our most distinguished and bestselling crime writers, creator of Dalglish and Pascoe and winner of the Golden Dagger and many other awards.

When we returned to Stanwix school, Reg and I rather traded on our notoriety for the rest of the term, as it made us known by the older classes. It became a bond between us, something we had gone through together.

But then, not long afterwards, our friendship was broken. In 1943, when I was aged seven, my father got another posting. He was being moved back over the border to Scotland. Reg and I promised to write to each other. We probably did, for a few weeks, but then the correspondence petered out and Carlisle began to fade from my mind.

Chapter Two

Fighting Hitler

We moved to Dumfries in 1943. I had no idea why. Were my parents homesick and wanting to return to Scotland? Was my father offered a better job? He was still doing the same thing, as a far as I was aware, working as a wages clerk attached to the RAF. He probably had no choice. It was war-time, so you did what you were told.

(Looking at 14MU's records, I now learn that in August 1940, the Carlisle depot took over space in Dumfries, which explains the move, mysterious though it was to me at the time.)

We lived in a house called Nancyville on the Annan Road, which sounds quite smart, as opposed to a council estate, but we didn't have the whole house, just rented part of it. The ground floor had been a shop but the front window had been boarded up and in it lived a disabled Polish airman. He'd had some sort of war injury, his face all burned, and looked rather frightening. We could hear him at night, banging around downstairs.

In the night could also be heard Peter, our cat, the first and only

Above: Me, left, rather hunched with asthma, in an itchy suit I hated, plus Marion, Annabelle, Johnny in Dumfries, 1944.

time I can remember having a family pet. Peter had disappeared in the fields behind our house for some weeks, presumed lost for ever, then returned one night half dead, dragging a trap in which his foot had been caught. One leg had to be amputated, but he lived on for many years, managing with three legs and a stump. The noise he made at night was a soft pad pad pad, followed by a thump of his gammy leg.

We only had two bedrooms. My parents slept in one while we four children slept in the other. Our bedroom was at the front and at night it was illuminated by the military convoys going along Annan Road towards England. The headlights would waken one of us up, who would start talking, and wake all the others.

As the oldest, I would say out loud 'One Two Three, no more talking, good night.' If anyone spoke after that, I had to say it all again. Strange how such a piddling, pointless little thing has stayed in my mind all these years.

Our mother made us say our prayers each evening before bed which always ended with 'And please God, look after all our soldiers, sailors and airmen.'

I went to Noblehill Primary School, just along the Annan Road, which was very handy and didn't need a bus. I fell in love there with a girl called Mary Ferguson. That's what it felt like. She was in my class, dark haired, pretty, and lived not far away. My tummy used to feel funny when I looked at her. I often walked past her house, just in the hope of catching sight of her. Oh the excitement when I was invited to her eighth birthday party, or could it have been her ninth. I definitely got into her house and we played pass the parcel and a musical game where you walked around in pairs, a boy and a girl, and when the music stopped, one particular pair had to kiss each other. Bliss.

At school we did a lot of knitting, each of us doing a square which would then be stitched together by the teacher to make blankets for our brave soldiers, sailors and airmen, whom God was busy looking after. Poor sods. My blanket square was always full of holes and taggles and wouldn't have kept anyone warm and safe. We saved waste paper to help fight Hitler and the Nazzzies, the ones not

20

Me, with very attractive buck teeth, with my cousin Sylvia, aged about seven, 1944.

keeping our boys safe. I was never clear how waste paper helped. Was it thrown at the Nazzies or turned into paper bombs? There were drawings in the comics showing piles of waste paper which we had saved and when the piles got to a certain height, they were marked 'Berlin'. That didn't make it any clearer, unless the piles of paper were for walking on.

We knew all about Hitler. He had a funny moustache, did a silly walk with one hand in the air, and had only one ball. As a child in the war, I don't remember Hitler as a scary figure, more a figure of fun. We knew nothing,. of course, about the concentration camps. We were more worried about Spies, people secretly watching what we were doing, who were usually thought to be old people we didn't like anyway, especially the ones who told us off.

In Dumfries, as in Carlisle, we had black-out curtains on our windows at home and a metal shelter under the kitchen table. We were issued with gas masks and ration books which bought very little. We never tasted real chocolate or proper sweets, just pretend sweets, made of what tasted like cardboard. My mother gave us what she said was mashed banana, which tasted quite nice, and we said yes, we like bananas, not knowing that they were mashed parsnips. Now and again, my father came home from work with a tin of fruit cocktail, containing bits of real fruit, what a treat that was. He'd got them from some American servicemen at his RAF station, so he said, though it might have well have been via the black market.

Even more special was to get hold of real chewing gum, which again needed contact with Americans. I managed this at first hand, or

21

first fingers. Convoys of American troops often passed along the Annan Road, throwing up clouds of dust. I would stand for hours by the side of the road, giving them the V for Victory sign. I couldn't manage on my own to form my fingers in the right arrangement, so my mother would do them for me, then I would rush out of the house and stand there, waving frantically at the Yankie jeeps and trucks till eventually one would throw out a packet of chewing gum. Other kids would appear from nowhere and we'd all scramble and fight each other in the gutter to grab the treasure. 'Got any gum, chum?' I can still hear myself shouting the words, with a Scottish accent of course.

Being at war seemed normal and ordinary. How life was, would always be. Being born in 1936, I had no memory of any pre-war life. I heard stories of people eating real oranges, real bars of milk chocolate, but couldn't believe it. Orange to us came in a bottle, thick stuff, which the clinic provided. Eggs were always dried. Our war-time comics were all skimpy, printed on cheap nasty paper with very few pages. One of my Cambuslang uncles gave me one of his pre-war comics which was so fat, with masses of pages and cartoons. I couldn't believe comics could ever be like that. But of course we needed paper for fighting Hitler.

At school one day, the teacher asked all those whose fathers were prisoners of war to stand up. When they did, they were all given food parcels. I was so jealous. I rushed home and complained loudly to my father that it wasn't fair, why wasn't he a prisoner of war.

Now I think about it, it was a good question. Not about being a POW I mean, but not fighting at the front. He was born in 1906, so probably a bit old by then to be called up, at least in the early years of the war. But he was part of the RAF anyway, on vital work, doing the wages for the airmen.

There was an Italian prisoner of war camp not far away. We would often see them, in trucks or in groups, being taken to work in the fields. They wore light brown tunics and light brown trousers. I remember the colour, despite being colour blind, because my mother bought me a little tunic jacket to wear which was almost the same colour. Kids at school shouted after me, Eye Tie, Eye Tie.

I got into one real fight in the playground, after someone had been calling me names. Perhaps for having come from England, rather than looking Italian. On that particular day, I'd had a terrible attack of asthma and felt awful, very weak, hunched and wheezing. I didn't have the energy for a fight, but this kid went on and on, pushing and pulling me, calling me names, till in the end, in anger and frustration, I managed to summon up courage and strength I never knew I had and flew into this kid like a wild animal, scratching and punching, screaming and shouting. Every other kid in the school had gathered round as the cry of 'Fight Fight Fight' had echoed round the playground. In the end, he backed away, frightened by what he had unleashed.

I always had asthma as a child. I can't remember not having it. Like the war, it had always been with me, a fact of my life. My mother and father both smoked, but I have never held that against them. Most grown-ups did. I once over-heard my grandmother Davies complaining that my mother had smoked over my cot, but I didn't understand the significance.

Doctors did prescribe various medicines, none of which ever gave much relief. There was a nasty powder I had to set fire to and inhale, which was supposed to help breathing, but it never did. Then there was a red rubber ball thing into which you put medicine and then squeezed it, and the spray went into your throat. I was given an allergy test, my arm covered with scores of pin pricks, like stamp perforations, but they didn't find any allergies, except dust.

One long summer holiday I was sent with my grandmother Brechin to the Highlands on a croft belonging to some distant relatives. The clean fresh Highland air was supposed to help my asthma. I did feel stronger and bigger, but this was mainly because on this croft were living two or three foster kids from the Glasgow slums, very small and scrawny. I'd always felt a midget, compared with Toddles, I mean Reggie, but for once I felt big.

I hated being with my Grandma. On the train there and back she insisted on telling total strangers that I had very bad asthma. She made me wear a special silk vest, next to my bare little chest, saying it would help my breathing. It did feel good, cool, clean and soothing.

During the war, I also spent another summer with my grandmother Davies in Glasgow at the very height of the bombing. I loved looking up at the enormous barrage balloons which were tethered in bits of open space, often just at the end of streets, held on ropes, but allowed to float in the sky. The most exciting part was rushing out of the house when the sirens sounded to take cover in the Anderson shelter in the garden. I would peer out at the night sky all lit up, hear the drone of Nazzie bombers heading for the Clyde shipyards, watch the sudden flashes of flames, hear the ack-ack guns trying to find the bombers, then would come a series of enormous explosions.

I enjoyed being in Glasgow in the middle of the bombing. It never struck me, till many years later, that it was a strange thing to do, sending a child from the safety of semi-rural Dumfries, where no bombing took place, to the centre of the Glasgow blitz. I think it was because my mother was ill, suffering from varicose veins. When she was in hospital, my father couldn't cope, and all fathers were useless in those days, so we were spread around relatives and neighbours.

Another time, when she was ill, I was for several weeks in charge of my younger sisters and brother, cooking for them and getting them to school. All I cooked was toast and boiled potatoes, which they hated, as I forced them to clean their plates. I must only have been aged eight or nine at the time. I also ran messages for neighbours, going on the bus into Dumfries with their shopping lists and ration coupons to buy their groceries. They would pay me a few pennies which I spent on marbles, comics or pretend sweets.

The first time I tasted real bananas was in Dumfries towards the end of the war. I was playing football in Noblehill Park when a cry started up amongst a group of kids nearest the road, then spread around the whole park. 'The Co-op's Got Bananas! The Co-op's Got Bananas!' Every kid took up the chant and then dashed from all corners of the park to run towards the Co-op. The word Co-op was pronounced 'Cope', as if it was one word. I didn't quite understand it at first when we moved from Carlisle.

Every customer was allowed only a small amount, so back at home, mothers would solemnly cut up a banana into small pieces and hand it round. I remember being sadly disappointed. Real bananas did not taste anything like parsnips.

At Noblehill School, I was quite high up in the class, except when it came to handwriting. I was constantly having to write out lines of letters and words over and over again. However careful I was, however long I took, my handwriting was still appalling. I was quite good at most lessons, for a boy, but of course the top of the class was always dominated by the girls. They seemed to fill the first five places in every subject, though the higher up the school we got, the more boys began to come through.

I have got one of my Noblehill report books from 1945-6, and it shows my class numbered 44 pupils and during that year, I came 11th, 5th and 4th in the class. At Stanwix Primary, there had been 49 in my class. I have only two reports from Stanwix and each one says 'Rather talkative!'

When I got to the age of eleven, and into the top class, I was led to believe I would be going on to Dumfries Academy, the secondary school for the so called cleverer children. That seemed to be what was expected. In Dumfries, the equivalent of the Eleven Plus was taken at twelve and called the Qualifying.

But in 1947, before I had even sat the entrance exam, we were on the move again - back to Carlisle. My father was returning once again to 14 MU. I don't know whether he chose to move back, or he had to. I just woke up one day and was told we were off.

My mother, sisters and brother went on the train while I travelled in the furniture van with my father. He sat at the front, with the driver, while I was at the back, with our meagre items of furniture. I was so excited when we set off. Being able to travel in any sort of car, even an old van, was looked upon as a special treat for children in the 1940's. I had been allowed to, being the oldest, much to the jealousy of my sisters and brother.

As the journey proceeded, and we got out into the country, going faster and faster, I began to feel sick, with all the bumping, and very cold with sitting in the open air, exposed to the wind. And also a bit scared. I realised I could not communicate with my father and the driver, should anything go wrong, such as another vehicle banging into us or being thrown right out of the van when we went over a particularly nasty bump in the road.

When we eventually reached our new home in Carlisle, I managed somehow to clamber out of the back of the van - and then was violently sick. Not an auspicious start to the beginning of what became my life proper in Carlisle.

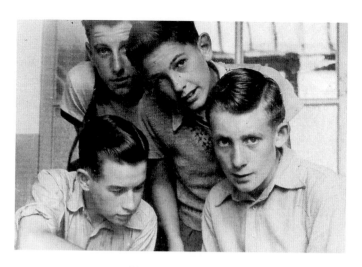

Chapter Three

Life at the Creighton

We had returned to St Ann's Hill in Carlisle, moving into 28 Caird Avenue, in the next street to where we had previously lived, the end of a little terrace of four houses. It backed on to the old allotments which had been used during the war by local people but now, two years after the war, had been allowed to grow wild and unattended. The ground was bumpy and overgrown, good for hiding in and games, with just enough flattish open space to play football. I soon made a hole in our back hedge for quick access.

I made contact again with my old friend Reggie, still living in Fraser Grove, and returned to my old school, Stanwix Primary. Although we had been away no more than four years, I had acquired a Scottish accent, so was immediately known as Scottie in the playground. I also found sums hard to understand. I had been good at them at Noblehill, but now in my class at Stanwix, when reciting our times-tables, and being cross examined on them, I couldn't get the

Above: On a school trip to France with the Creighton, 1951. I'm at the back on right, standing with Ian Kenning. Alastair McFadden and Colin Cuthbert are at the front

hang of it. For some reason, they were recited in a different way from Scotland, yet of course they were the same. So much of learning was by rote, the whole class reciting the same things aloud, over and over, so you picked up things parrot fashion, without quite understanding them. I had remembered Miss Tinn, because of her unusual surname and also her grey hair and bun and fearsome manner.

It slowly began to dawn on me that the class had divided itself into little cliques. The children going to Carlisle Grammar School and the Carlisle and County High School were forming their own little circles, cutting themselves off socially and intellectually from the also-rans, the second class citizens, the ones who apparently had not passed the Merit, which was what Carlisle's Eleven Plus exam was called.

In Dumfries, I had not yet sat my exam, but in England, the top class at all primary schools had already taken their Eleven Plus and each child had recently been informed of the results and knew where they were going - not just for the next five years, but for life. If you didn't go to the grammar school, your chances of any further education, and therefore a good job in life, were nil. That was it, for ever.

I didn't quite understand what was going on, the system, the terminology, the names of the schools people were talking about, or the long term implications, but I was aware that some sort of important divisions had taken place, which was why the chosen children were already segregating themselves.

My parents knew even less about the system than I did. My mother, in all her years in Carlisle, never really understood Carlisle anyway, the names of places, streets and institutions. It always remained a mystery to her. Getting on the C3 or C4 from St Ann's to the Town Hall, going to Orams or Robsons the butchers, to Liptons or the Maypole Dairy, into the Market for vegetables, perhaps to Binns for clothes or household things on special occasions, that was about all that really mattered to her, and even then, she still got lost.

But either she or someone at Stanwix School must eventually have alerted the education authorities to the fact that I had not been allocated to a secondary school. The Grammar School was full, so she was told, and had a reserve list, so that was it. I would have to go

The Creighton School today.

to Lowther Street, one of the sec. moderns.

One day I found myself sitting in the headmaster's office at a big school called the Creighton School in Strand Road. I had been set my own little exam. I can't remember what sort of questions there were, but I remember it being strange that I was on my own. The headmaster was tall and thin with sleeked down hair. His name was Mr Boulton. Funny spelling, so I thought, with a u, not as in Bolton Wanderers.

After my little exam paper, he asked me what I wanted to do in life and I said be a professional footballer. I had taken the question to be about my fantasy job in life, not what I expected to be. It must have struck him as amusing, this small, weedy, asthmatic child having such an ambition.

I don't remember his reply, or being told the result of my exam, but in September, 1947, I started at the Creighton School. I wore a dark blue blazer and a red and blue tie, a proper uniform, which appeared to make it a cut above Robert Ferguson or Lowther Street, secondary schools which had no uniform.

I've just looked up my school reports from the Creighton School, which I have kept for every year, mainly because they were in the same Report Book which you had to cover with brown paper and carry throughout your school career, if not through life. I see that the headmaster who signed my reports for the first two years was Mr

29

Bainbridge. Mr Boulton did not come till my third year. So is my memory playing tricks? Were they both tall and thin with sleeked down hair? I've obviously got that wrong. It must have been Mr Bainbridge who first saw me, but Mr Boulton has stayed in my mind longer, hence the confusion.

Another confusion is my name. On the front of my Report Book it says 'HUNTER DAVIES'. Inside I am sometimes E.H. Davies, Edward Hunter Davies and even Edward Hunter-Davies.(We did actually have a double barrelled boy in our class, Norman Heeley-Creed, but his was genuine. Who says the Creighton wasn't a quality school?) I have gone through life with this problem, and usually never reveal that Hunter is not strictly my true, first christian name.

I was christened Edward Hunter Davies, the Hunter bit being a long established family name, hence my father, John Hunter Davies. He was always called John but for some reason, right from birth, I was always known as Hunter. Why they didn't put it as my first christian name, I'll never know.

It came as a big surprise the first time I learned the truth. I was at Stanwix School and a school nurse was looking for nits and she said, 'Edward, come here.' I looked around, wondering who the Edward was. We didn't have an Edward in the class, soppy name, so I was getting ready to giggle. I was hauled out in the end, still refusing to believe it was me.

This kept on happening throughout my school life. All teachers and pupils would know that I was called Hunter, but on

City of   Carlisle
EDUCATION COMMITTEE

COUNCIL
CERTIFICATE

This is to certify that

Edward Hunter· Davies

a pupil of the *Creighton* School was awarded the Carlisle Council Certificate in the year *1950* being placed in the *1st class Honours* Division passing with ~~credit in the following subjects~~ *distinction in Algebra, Geometry, Scripture, English Language & Literature.*

Signed on behalf of the Education Committee,

Head Master

Director of Education

30

official forms, like medical reports, the Edward would suddenly pop out, some bossy nurse trying to be matey and personal would say it out loud and I would hate her.

I now love being called Hunter. Partly because I've never met another person with it as a first name, apart from in the USA, where surnames as first names are common. But it still leads to confusions the first time I give it, in hotels or restaurants, where it gets written down as David Hunter. Once people have got it right, they do tend to remember it. Usually, I deny I have or ever had another first name.

Many years later, when Paul McCartney was staying with us in Portugal, it came out by chance what my real first name was. He burst out laughing, going off to the lavatory with his guitar. He then came back and sang me a little song called 'There you go, Eddie'. I don't know why he mocked. The world knows he was in fact christened James Paul McCartney. So, see you Jimmy.

The Creighton School seemed to be half way between the Grammar School and a secondary modern, where all the Eleven Plus failures went. Not thickos, exactly, but obviously not quite up to the standard of the Brain Box boys who had passed for the Grammar or the Brain Box girls who went on to the High School. There was a sister school to the Creighton called the Margaret Sewell, in an adjoining building, which was the school to which my twin sisters went. One of them, Annabelle was on the reserve list for the High School, so we were told later, but Marion had only managed the reserve list for the Maggie Anne, as it was known, so it was decided to keep them togther, as they were twins, and send them to the same school. My younger brother Johnny, when he came to the Eleven Plus, did not make any reserve lists and was shunted off to Kingstown School.

Carlisle's tripartite system, with three layers of secondary schools, was an unusual arrangement, so I realised many years later. In most towns, there were only two. I have also just discovered, which I never knew at the time, just how few children aged eleven did pass the Merit in Carlisle in the 1940's and 1950's.

In a 1958 booklet, issued by Carlisle Corporation, about the Local Government of the City and County Borough of Carlisle, it states that the top eighth each year went to the Grammar or the High School while the next eighth went to the Creighton and the Margaret Sewell 'where the education is inclined to be scientific, technical and commercial, but is of the same standard as the Grammar and the High School'. So in other words, $12\frac{1}{2}\%$ went to the Grammar and High, the next $12\frac{1}{2}\%$ to the Creighton and Margaret Sewell, while the vast majority, some 75%, were consigned to the secondary moderns. I felt a gulf between the Creighton and the Grammar, so the next gap, between the sec mods and the chosen few, must have seemed enormous. The Creighton not only had uniform, but did French and played rugby, three signs that the school had pretensions. One half of the school, the A stream, could go on to take the General Certficate of Education O levels at sixteen, but there was no sixth form. Everyone, whether they had passed any sort of exam or not, left the school and started work at either fifteen or sixteen.

I was lucky, in a way, that in Carlisle such a school as the Creighton existed, but intellectually and socially, we knew we were inferior to the Grammar. Down the road at the Grammar, so I learned from Reggie and other friends who had gone there, masters wore gowns, indicating they had degrees, which very few had at the Creighton, and Greek, Latin and German were taught as well as French. The names of their classes had strange names, like the Fifth Remove, and school work got marked not in numbers or percentages but with Alpha Minus or Beta Plus Plus. Their building appeared very old and ancient, covered in ivy, while our school was red brick and modern. We did though have an excellent gym, extensive playing fields and lots of space. I went into 1T, the letter standing for our form teacher, Mr Thomson, whereas the other half, went into 1P which stood for Mr Potter. We had been divided at random, not on merit. I was pleased because Mr Thomson seemed a nicer, kinder man than Mr Potter. In the playground, I was again called Scottie, as my accent had remained from our stay in Dumfries.

At the top of the school, in the Fifth Form, were enormous boys, some with signs of a moustache and the beginning of beards, proper, hulking, frightening looking boy-men. Even in the first year, there were boys already about twice my size, such as one called Swanny who seemed like a giant.

At the end of the first year, we sat an exam and the top half went into 2A and the other half into 2B. Almost everyone stayed in these streams, as they moved up through the school, which meant that those in the B form would never sit a GCE and would leave school at fifteen without any qualifications. Those in the B stream became apprentice electricians or plumbers, worked in shops, or did clerical jobs. Those in the A stream, who stayed on and managed a few GCE O Levels, went into places like Laings the builders as trainee draughtsmen. That seemed to be the most desirable job for Creightonians to aspire to.

Many of the male teachers had recently come out of the Forces, having done short term teacher training courses which were made simpler and quicker after the War to encourage men into teaching. Most of them seemed to have passed few exams themselves, judging by the lack of any letters after their names on the speech day programmes. I never ever heard our French teacher speak French. I suspected he had never sat a French exam, but had simply been roped in to teach it, as no one else would do it. He would make us read out aloud, and tell us if our pronunciation was good or bad, without any French ever passing through his own lips.

But there were some excellent, enthusiastic teachers whose lessons I grew to love as I went up the school. Dotty Watson taught English and I remember once going out to visit her at her home in Kirkoswald. Seems a creepy, teacher's pet sort of thing to do, not like me, or my image of myself, the one I have retained all these years. Perhaps I just happened to be passing, and knocked on her door, though why I would be passing through Kirkoswald seems unlikely as for so many years the countryside around Carlisle was a foreign land to me, just as it was to my mother. Then there was the history teacher who was so dynamic, so enthusiastic, who would rush into lessons armed with work sheets and new information he had just researched or mugged up. He made a great impression on me - yet I'm now struggling to remember his name. It will come to me in a minute, or when I dig out my old school reports and see his signature. He was brilliant on social history, on the history of railways, the industrial revolution, the rise of the trade unions, an interest that has never left me. Not so good on political history. Now I look at my school report, I see his initials were J.M.W. Mr Wilson?

The ogre, the teacher everyone feared and loathed, was Mr Garrigan who taught maths. He was small, ugly, bespectacled, very sarcastic. He had apparently been a good rugby player, a scrum half by his build, and was still a big cheese in Cumberland Rugby Union, not that that was of any interest, as I hated rugby. I had only been at the school a few months when he called me out for some reason and made some catty comment about my accent, asking where I had come from. I said Dumfries. He asked which part. I said the outskirts of Dumfries. 'I never knew Dumfries had skirts.'

A really stupid, obvious, banal joke, but of course the whole class laughed uproariously, keeping in with Garry, enjoying my discomfort, glad that they were not being picked upon. I used to dread his lessons so much that I often bunked off, sitting in the drying room of the cloakroom in the dark, along with a few other pathetic specimens, in order to miss his lessons, shaking in fear in case we got found out.

He seemed to me a poor teacher, who ruled by fear and ridiculed anyone who was slow or stupid or simply had failed to understand the theorems he had so badly explained. About the third year, it all began to dawn on me, which I think was thanks to me, not him. It just suddenly seemed to make sense and I actively enjoyed doing algebra and geometry, something I had never expected.

For the first year, I turned up for games, which meant rugby, even though I was always put with the weedy, the overweight or the sickly, the ones who were forced to play amongst themselves behind the goals while the games teacher devoted himself to the thugs and morons who played on the proper pitch. I still had terrible asthma, always wheezing and puffing, so in the end, I got a medical certificate from the doctor and for the rest of my career at the Creighton I was permanently excused games.

I still did gym which was enough of an ordeal. In the showers, bigger kids would flick wet towels at you, which really did hurt, and then very soon, as we went up the school, they were flaunting their pubic hair and their big willies, walking up and down the showers displaying themselves. One trick was to pull their cock back between their legs to make it look as though they had a hairy fanny, then pretend to speak in a girl's voice, asking if anyone fancied them. This was all very embarrassing and humiliating for pathetic specimens like me, with not a pubic hair in sight, far less a willy you could do anything with.

I was still in short trousers till I was at least fourteen, perhaps even fifteen, which was another source of humiliation. Boys, even quite big boys, all wore short trousers in those days and woollen socks which hung at half mast, like Just William's. Having bare legs in the winter was agony. I was always getting my thighs chaffed, partly through not wearing underpants and the pee dripping when I went to the lavatory. I didn't know why I didn't have any underpants. I did get them now and again for Christmas, from aunts in Scotland, along with vests, which I always considered the most useless presents ever.

In the playground, a popular game was to go around grabbing other boys by the balls, which was particularly uncomfortable if you didn't have any underpants. It wasn't sexual, not that I was aware of, just a way of inflicting pain on others. We did make jokes about homos, without knowing what they did to each other. We would shout 'backs to the wall' when boys assumed to be effeminate came near us, but still didn't know what it all meant. There was a scruffy old potter who lived in Caldewgate called Paddy Mason who was said to be one of them, you know, a homo, so you shouldn't go near him. Potter was not someone who worked with clay but the Carlisle term for a tramp or rag and bone man.

By the third year at the Creighton, several boys who had appeared normal and in fact quite eager in the first year had given up on school, just messed around in class or absented themselves from lessons, stole things and committed various minor acts of vandalism. I was fascinated by them. I half admired their bravery and bravado, even though I knew that most things they did were really stupid. I was such a scaredy pants, keeping in with authority, being polite to teachers, doing what I was told. They seemed to get such a buzz, such excitement, out of stealing from shops, such as Dinkies from

Woolies, then giving them away. They tended to be the bigger, more sexually advanced boys, but not always the most stupid. I was very friendly with one called Vinny who was just as good as me at lessons in the first two years, till he gave up, maintaining he was being picked upon, so what was the point.

During one week-end when the school was closed, someone broke in and forced open the headmaster's office door. Petty cash was stolen from a desk, several bits of furniture and windows were smashed and a small fire started.

On Monday morning, when we arrived for school, we all stood around in shock horror, staring at the damage, convinced it must have been real professional thieves. In the cloakroom later that morning, bunking off from Garry and his Maths, I found Vinny was also hiding there - and he told me that he had done it. Boasted he'd done it. I asked him why, and he said because he felt like it, he hated the school, wanted to get his own back. He described exactly how he had done it, what a laugh it had been, what good fun, though he had been shitting himself most of the time. He was soon found out and disappeared for a couple of terms, presumably to an approved school.

When Teddy Boys came in, Creighton had its fair share, some of them headcases who carried razors who would hang around the Town Hall after school, looking for rivals to beat up. There was a ginger headed one I was terrified of, who'd left school, or been expelled, who used to hang around the school entrance in his brothel creepers, drape jacket, greased back DA hair cut, swinging his chain, looking for any goody-goodies to thump if they happened to look at him the wrong way, or even just looked at him

The stars of the school, the ones most admired, were of course the sports stars, as they always were and always will be at every secondary school, for boys as well as girls, at least up to a certain age. In our class we had a boy called Brian Davison who was an excellent runner. He seemed to do it so effortlessly, winning everything on sports day. He was dark haired, well built and handsome, which made everyone really jealous, though he was in fact a very nice bloke, not at all boastful, quiet and conscientious. I lost touch with him, after the age of sixteen when he and I had left the Creighton, so I was very surprised many years later, and most impresssed, to read in the Cumberland News that he had become Director of Carlisle City Council's Environmental Health Department.

The clever ones, the swots in our class, were Dobbo and Barker, who seemed to come top in most lessons. I hated them most of all for being neat fuckers. Their essays and sums were always immaculately presented while their technical drawing work, a subject I hated, was stunning.

I said 'fucker' there, but at the time I didn't. I don't remember using such obscene or profane language as a school boy, nor did most other people, even the thugs and thickos. Swearing was minimal, the f and c words rarely used, even amongst close friends. Talking dirty and crude, that was different and very common. By the third and fourth year, dirty books like Hank Jansen's were being passed around, or drawings and photos of naked women which had been torn out of Health and Efficiency. Sexual things were constantly talked about, but the language used was slang rather than four letter swearing. A girl was a tart, bewer or bint, her vagina was a minge, boys boasted how they were going to fin some tart and get a sticky finger. Most of it fantasy talk of course. Instead, when they got hard ons, boys had to be content to toss themselves off. I can't recall hearing the word wanker, not in Carlisle in the 1950's.

I remember being rather disgusted at school dinners one day when we were having bakewell tart and custard and two older boys at my table were complaining about how thin and meagre the custard was. They each said their cum was better and thicker than that, boasting how much they could produce in one session. I was still at that stage pre-pubic and rather revolted by such crude talk.

Gadgy was a bloke, of any age. Scran was food. Chaw was a mate, a friend, as in Hiya Chaw. Nash was to go or run quickly. Radge meant someone who was daft or stupid. Shan was to be embarrassed and could be transitive or intransitive. You could shan someone, or be shanned to deeth or an incident could be a queer shan. Marra also meant mate, but was more common amongst people from Worky than Carlisle.

I still use some of these words, such as shan and scran, but I'm not sure how you spell them as I never saw them written down, except of course for Worky meaning Workington.

Worky was also the name of a football game we played when we didn't have a proper pitch, taking turns at kicking into the same goals. When you missed the goal, and it was a bye, or a goalkick, you then had to defend while the other side kicked in.

The woodwork and metalwork rooms at the Creighton were well equipped, as you might expect in a school where many boys were going to become craftsmen. I was totally useless at either activity, but at least no one seemed to mind or tell you off or cared how long you took. The woodwork and metalwork teachers were silent, surly, bull-like men who seemed to spend their time slaving over their own creations rather than teaching. Like the PE teachers, if you gave them cheek or annoyed them, you would get a good hard slap round the ears.

I spent about three long, deadly boring years in metalwork before I was able to drop it. By that time I had finally completed my Companion Set, something most boys at the Creighton finished in one term. This consisted of an iron poker, a dust pan and a pair of tongs, each with a little hook, which hung together on a little stand, hence they were a companion set, jolly useful for mothers when they were setting or tending the coal fire, which of course every Carlisle household had.

Mine must be in pristine condition, wherever it is now, for I never saw it being used for the purpose it was intended. We did have a fire, so my companion set would have been useful, but the poker I made was bent and knobbly, the pan had holes in it, the tongs did not fit together so were useless for picking anything up, while the stand never stood but always fell over.

The Creighton School was meant to provide a technical education, for boys not quite bright enough to make the Grammar, but that side of it was all wasted on me.

Chapter Four

Father Frets

When I was about twelve, and had not long started at the Creighton, my father began staggering. He would come home from the Redfern, the pub nearest to our house in St Ann's Hill, holding on to the gates and hedges in Caird Avenue to steady himself. Naturally, the neighbours assumed he was drunk. He went out only once a week to the Redfern, on Saturday with some of his friends from 14 MU, and didn't really drink a lot. We never had drink in the house, except at Christmas when my mother would buy a bottle of VP British Sherry and a bottle of Egg Nog from the County Hotel off licence, just beside the railway station. She kept the bottles in the cocktail cabinet in our front parlour and would offer a glass to visitors over Christmas time or more usually New Year's Day. Being Scottish, Hogmanay mattered more to us than Christmas Day.

Above: My father, seated, already in a wheelchair, plus, standing, left to right, sister Annabelle, mother, me, aged 18, sister Marion, and at front, brother Johnny, in Caird Avenue, Carlisle, 1954.

'Cocktail cabinet' and 'parlour' makes our council house seem ever so smart, but lots of people had cocktail cabinets, made of shiny cheap wood with glass doors in which one's best ornaments would be kept. My mother's treasures included three little brass monkeys crouched in different poses, to represent See no Evil, Hear no Evil and Speak no Evil. She also had a pair of brass candlesticks and two fancy coloured glass goblets which were kept purely for show, as if they were precious objects, family heirlooms handed down. I think they had been prizes won at some fairground at Troon or Rothesay when my parents had been courting. I always wished my father had gone for the goldfish instead.

Cocktail cabinets never contained cocktails, whatever they were. They were mainly seen as status symbols in respectable working class homes. I suspect that many of the computers you see today are hardly ever used for computing, or even for writing and printing out information. They are there for games, but also to show status, that parents are in touch, up-to-date.

Also in this parlour, which was the little front room to the left of the front door, was a piano. A very old, beat up one, which no one could play, though my sisters had for a time been sent to lessons at sixpence an hour.

Over the following year, my father's staggering got worse, and his hands began to shake as well. No one seemed to know what was the cause and it began to make him very bad tempered. I had a tremendous row with him once over a piece of fretwork which he had insisted I help him with. He was not at all handy in the house, no more than I was, but got it into his head that he would make some book-ends, despite the fact that we owned very few books. The half a dozen we had were cheap medical books and gardening books, bought with tokens through the Daily Express.

He'd bought a fretwork saw and I had to hold the wood, while he sawed away, following a plan of the book-ends to be. Sounds like a bit of father-son bonding, but I doubt if that entered his mind. I can't remember as a child doing anything with him, or being taken anywhere, as we never went on family holidays or outings. Fathers in those days did not do much with their children, nor did they push

Our house in Caird Avenue as it is today.

prams in the street, but I was the only child, before the others came along as I have snaps of me aged about three or four on the beach at Troon in Scotland.

Because of his shaking hands, the saw kept on slipping, and he blamed me, shouting at me for being clumsy and stupid. He had begun to shout at me a lot, mainly telling me to 'pipe down', complaining that my voice gave him a headache. I was a noisy child, I was aware of that, and at school I was always being told off for being too talkative. Fifty odd years later, I haven't changed much. My wife still tells me to sit down, stop fidgeting, why can't I be still, stop nattering, keep quiet, like a normal person.

In the end, with shouting at me, and his hands shaking, he split the special piece of fret wood, making it useless. He threw it at me, and the saw, blaming me for what had happened, then he sort of collapsed on the floor as his legs gave way.

I thought it was just his bad temper, not that there was anything wrong with him, so I slammed out of the kitchen door, saying that was it, I was off, and never coming back. I reappeared a few minutes later, stepped over him as he still lay on the kitchen floor, went upstairs and packed some clothes in a big hankie. I slung it over my shoulder, like Dick Whittington, and stormed out again, saying they would never see me again, goodbye. The twins, who had had to watch this scene, were in tears, and my little brother Johnny was very upset, the three of them thinking it was true. I was running away for good. My mother might also have been in tears, not fearful of me running away, but fearful of what was really wrong.

It took some time for multiple sclerosis to be confirmed, after various tests, different explanations and several false hopes. When it was diagnosed, its progress was rampant and his physical deterioration very quick. He was discharged from 14MU and given an ugly clock as his leaving present.

He was soon unable to get up the stairs to his bedroom so a single bed was put in the front parlour and the piano removed. When he went out, which he did for about another year, he had to be pushed in a pushchair. I often had to do it, being the oldest and biggest, and I hated it. Not just the shan of having an invalid father, but it was hellish to push, as he was so heavy and the wheelchair so clumsy. He liked being pushed up Belah Road, which was a steep hill, up to the Redfern where he would sit outside while people would bring him the odd pint, if he was lucky.

Outside, in public, he was cheerful and friendly, waved his hands to people getting off the bus, even when he couldn't quite see them as his eyes began to deteriorate as well. At home, inside the house, he grew more and more bad tempered, throwing his meals at my mother, if he didn't happen to like what she had made for him.

One of my jobs was to fill in his football pools for him and then on Saturdays at five o'clock, sitting with him as we listened to Sports Report on the radio, filling in the scores in the Daily Express, then checking how many draws he had got on the treble chance. None was usually the answer, or not enough to win anythng. I would be blamed for his lack of success, that I'd got the scores wrong. Every Saturday today, when I hear that familiar tune which introduces Sports Report, and then listen to the voice of James Alexander Gordon reading out the results, I think of my father.

The Redfern at St Ann's Hill where my father had a drink.

On Sundays, I would read out to him the quiz from the Sunday Post, as he prided himself on being good at general knowledge. I moaned and groaned at having to do these little jobs, which was unfair, as I got off so lightly. My mother got the brunt of his bad temper and did most of the looking after as did my sisters, when they got a bit older. My sister Marion was particularly good with him. When he'd thrown down his meal, she would tell him off, threaten him with no more food, and he would apologise and say sorry.

Of course I felt sympathy for him. Someone who had been so fit and active and sociable, made immobile in his forties, but at the time I was more interested in my own life. He hadn't after all been such a big presence in my life, as far as I could remember. Perhaps he had been ill for far longer than I realised.

And yet, at the same time, it seemed sort of normal, how life was, that was what happened, and we just got used to it. I don't recall thinking our life was much different from those around us on the estate. No one seemed to have any more material possessions, or took holidays, or ran a car. Reggie's family life seemed much the same as ours, though their house was neater and tidier. Mrs Hill always made me take my shoes off and wash my hands whenever I was allowed in to play cards with Reg. Our house might have been a bit messy, with

43

clothes strewn around, shirts and frocks hanging from the picture rail in the living room, the one and only bathroom towel always wet and grubby, but at least no one told you off for being untidy, to wash your hands or put your things away.

My father got no help from anyone, and hardly any medical treatment or other forms of care and support. For a while, once a month or so, an ambulance came and took him to the Cumberland Infirmary for physio, but he hated it and it did him no good and they soon gave up. Once a year he went for a week to some sort of residential home at Grange over Sands, respite care for my mother, to give her a break, but he hated that as well. The moment my mother appeared at his bedside he would mutter 'Get me the hell out of here'.

No nurses came to help bathe and clean him, although he was a heavy man, hard to manoeuvre, or attend to his sores which soon started with lying in bed all day. My mother didn't have a hoist or a stair lift or an invalid's shower or any of the other facilities which such invalids are entitled to today, supplied by the National Health or other agencies. There was of course no MS Society. He had just been dumped in our parlour and forgotten by society.

His friends and neighbours, such as they were, with whom he used to go to the pub, ceased to visit. Some of them had been promoted, moved to a better area, able to buy their own house. Not long before he took ill, my father had been before some sort of Civil Service board and emerged as a Higher Executive Officer. That might have been why we moved back to Carlisle, with the prospects of promotion. Perhaps there would have been more advancement to come, had he not got MS.

I know something about living with MS today because by a terrible irony, life repeated itself, not for me, but my sister Annabelle. Having helped nurse my father, her own husband Roger, also a civil servant, was struck down with MS when he too got into his forties. Life and the social services had moved on by then and the care and support system they were able to call upon was excellent, helpers and nurses calling all day long, every modern facility in his bedroom to ease his physical discomfort, lots of grants and allowances available. In 1950, there seemed to be nothing. If anything did exist, my mother never knew about them.

As for money, I don't know how she managed. I presume when he retired through ill health, he got some sort of pension, but my mother had four young children to provide for through their most expensive years for food and clothes. Her total income was about £3 a week - £1 of which went on rent. She never moaned or complained. If the topic ever came up, she would say 'Oh, lots of money, I've got lots of money.' Which was a total lie.

Every Monday there was always pandemonium in our house, as if Monday was a surprise, she had not seen it coming. We all needed bus money and dinner money to get to school, and she never had enough, or never had the right change. Chairs would be overturned, drawers emptied as the twins and I ran round the house, searching for any lost pennies.

We paid for our school dinners, as I can remember handing in the money each Monday morning. There might have been some embryo system of income support, or free school meals for households with no wage earners, but no one told her how to apply. My mother didn't understand about the English Eleven Plus exam, how the Ribble buses operated, had never heard of Silloth, got lost going down Botchergate, so how could she cope with the suits at Carlisle City Council Social Services Department. She had other things on her mind. Apart from my father's condition, she herself was in poor health, suffering from varicose vein ulcers and eventually had an operation. My mother's escape was reading. Although we didn't own any books, apart from the handful of reference books, there were always library books lying around. Each week she got out the maximum number, all of them novels. She loved Somerset Maugham, Galsworthy, A J Cronin and, best of all, Dickens.

I can see her now, standing at the kitchen stove, stirring the mince, which was slowly drying out and about to burn, turning over the pages of Nicholas Nickleby or Oliver Twist, reading aloud her favourite bits and laughing to herself. She usually read standing up, having so little time in her life to sit down. No wonder she had problems with her varicose veins. Every year, she re-read all of Dickens, and all her other favourite authors.

45

She hardly ever sat down with us, but remained in the kitchen, bringing plates back and forwards. Usually mince and potatoes, sometimes potatoes on their own, often just toast. The teapot was permanently stewing. 'I've heard tea is very good for you,' she would say, pouring out her twentieth cup of the morning.

In the kitchen itself was the coal-hole, a dark little concrete pantry with its own door. The coalman would have to walk through the kitchen with the bags of coal on his back then empty them inside the coal-hole, which meant there was instantly coal dust everywhere. The coalman had a horse and cart as many delivery people did in the forties and fifties. The fruit and veg man was Mr Shaw, a farmer from Cargo, and he also had a horse. My mother would make me rush outside when she saw any horse manure as she'd heard it was good for the garden. I was always embarrassed, picking up horse shit, which was a waste of time anyway as there was nothing growing in our garden.

Next to the kitchen was an outside wash house with a gas boiler tub which had to be lit for the water to be heated. She would soak and then thump the clothes with a wooden dolly, scrub them on a wash board, wring out the water with a hand wringer, then hang the washing out on the line. Usually having to take them in almost at once, as it started raining. We had no drying facilities, apart from a clothes-horse which would be draped in front of the coal fire. The steam and mist from the damp clothes, allied with the smoke from our fire which never drew properly, would make me choke the minute I entered the room. Our street was always dusty anyway with the soot from the railway engines at Kingmoor sidings.

Hot water for the bathroom was heated by some sort of back boiler behind the coal fire, which was very inefficient. Traditionally the working classes of the time had one hot bath a week. I can't remember having any. I hated our bathroom, so cold, damp, cheerless. There was no heating in the house, apart from the coal fire. When I was really ill with asthma, and forced to stay all day in my bed in my horrible bedroom which I shared with Johnny, my mother would bring up a tray of hot coals and put them in my little fireplace and let the downstairs fire go out. She couldn't afford two fires.

I loved the sight of the hot embers arriving and the little fireplace being lit, suddenly making my bedroom marginally comfortable, slightly warm and passably attractive. I would sit up and turn over the pages of my stamp album, looking into each stamp, imagining lives in all the different countries, or study the pages of my football album, where I had stuck in photos of my favourite players, till slowly, my wheezing would subside and perhaps even stop. I discovered quite early on, without exactly working it out, that while all the medicines and potions failed, if only I could take my mind off my wheezing, somehow distract my mind, my body would start to recover. By then, the fire would be totally out, and the room freezing, but with luck I would have fallen asleep.

Our bedroom floor was covered in linoleum. In winter time, it would be absolutely freezing, so you devised a system of somehow getting from under the blankets straight into your clothes, without touching the lino, otherwise your bare feet would be left there, stuck for ever to the lino.

This was our house in Carlisle in 1950, normal life so I assumed, for everyone. Writing it down now makes it sound more like 1850. At the time, I didn't write it down or remark on it or even think about it. And if asked about it, I would have said I'm having a very happy childhood, thank you very much.

Chapter Five

Come on You Blues

Slowly, through the 1950's, families around us got electric immersion heaters in their water tanks, which provided reliable hot water. They put extra plugs in the rooms, so electric fires could be plugged in. The more affluent acquired a fridge, a phone and a TV. We never had any of these things, until the 1960's. In 1953, for the Coronation, there was one local family with a TV. My sisters, being friends of theirs, were allowed to stand in their front garden, looking through the front window to catch a glimpse of the lovely Queen.

My father's income had come to a halt, so there were no improvements, refurbishments or DIY being done. But we did have a radio, which was the main source of entertainment for most families of the 1950's.

Throughout most of my childhood and teenage life it was connected to the overhead light bulb socket in the living room, the only way it could be plugged in, which was highly dangerous, as the wires became frayed with constantly being pulled in and out. We couldn't of course have a light on while listening to the radio. I quite enjoyed listening in the dark to the Saturday play or Paul Temple with my

Above: Creighton School trip to France. I'm third from the right.

mother.

My father loved ITMA, and would repeat all the popular phrases and smile, but I was never a fan, couldn't see why it was thought so funny. Perhaps I was too young. It was aimed more at my parents' generation. I didn't think much of Educating Archie either and found the idea of a ventriloquist on radio very strange. When the Goon Show started, I adored it, copied all the silly voices, as all my friends did, while my father couldn't see the joke at all.

My mother did her best with the house, despite having no money, most of her energies going into repainting the kitchen walls which she did constantly, always in lurid colours with cheap paint, end-of-line pots bought in Woolworths. The pots would usually run out after one wall, or half a wall, so mid way up a wall, deep purple would turn into bright green. The kitchen walls were bare brick, unplastered, so the effect of the paint was to make them glaring and brutal. You could see visitors shielding their eyes when they entered the back door. I was supposed to do the garden, cut the grass with a useless rusty handmower, trim the front privet hedge and keep down the weeds. There were some immaculate front lawns in Caird Avenue, but our garden always looked a dump, giving totally the wrong impression, as if we were potters not a family with a mother who read Dickens.

I picked up my love of going to the public library from my mother. It was in Tullie House, where the smart, prize winning museum now is. The building, as everyone in Carlisle knows, is a Jacobean gem, built 1689, but from 1893 it had housed the City Library. It also had a museum, very old fashioned, with glass cases, stuffed animals, Roman remains, daft collections which had been donated to the City. Children visited it with their school, and told not to talk or touch things. I found it very dreary at the time, but now I greatly miss such museums. Far too many modern ones have gone madly audio-visual and interactive, strong on display but with very few actual objects.

I loved going to the Library which consisted of a reference library as well as an adult and a children's library. Moving up from the children's library was a huge stage in life, like going into long

The Ref at Tullie House

pants, transferring from primary to secondary school, or the Cubs into the Scouts.

I can still smell the polish and wood. I came across the same smell once in Caracas in Venezuela, and immediately thought I was back in Tullie House. In my mind's eye, the librarians had buns and were grey haired and fearsome, telling you off if you breathed too loudly or ran around. You were only allowed a limited number of books, so if you came across any Just Williams or Biggles books, newly returned, which you hadn't read, you hid them in a far corner or on the wrong shelves, hoping they would be there next time, or so your friends could find them. The Buns, of course, over their specs, were usually watching, and smartly put them back.

I don't think I have ever loved books as I loved Just William books. They removed me completely from my world, caused me to choke with laughter, roll around holding my stomach. Oh I do hope that children reading Harry Potter today get the same enjoyment I did from Just William.

As we all know, the life of William, in his Home Counties posh house, with maids and tennis courts, was light years away from life in Caird Avenue, but that didn't matter, no more than it worried us

Bramwell Evens, Romany on Children's Hour.

that the Wizard and Hotspur featured public schools, fags and tuck shops, which were equally remote from our own experiences. Did we long to be there, to escape, was that the attraction? I don't think so. They were exciting stories, so we thought at the time, or funny stories in the case of Just William. We did identify with William himself, if not his social context, with his socks hanging down, being told off all the time, his relationships with adults and of course having his own little gang, their schemes and plots. Our gangs in St Ann's Hill had much the same object, either to defeat or confound our supposed enemies or how to get money to buy sweets.

I played football in the lotties behind our house most days after school, despite my asthma, puffing and panting, coming in red in the face at precisely 6.45 to listen to Dick Barton, Special Agent. The sound of the signature tune coming through an open window was enough to have children stopping at once what they were doing and haring home.

I also listened to Children's Hour - on the Scottish Home Service, which our wireless was always tuned into. In the morning, we got delivered the Scottish edition of the Daily Express and the Sunday Post on Sunday. Lots of people in Carlisle still get Scottish papers, being a Border town, with so many families having migrated, but I can't remember there being other Scottish families on our estate, so when playing in the lotties or the street next day, and I talked about Tammy Troot or Doon at the Mains, or repeated Jimmy Logan's favourite phrase, 'sausages is the boys' no-one knew what I was on about. Now I think about it, it was a particularly stupid phrase, but then all catch phrases are, once their life has run its course.

51

I loved Norman and Henry Bones, the boy detectives, who were on the main stream Children's Hour, and wandering with Romany or Nomad which were nature programmes, during and after the war, about two children being taken on a country walk, and having things pointed out and spotted.

I never knew, in all those years of listening, that the man behind Romany had been living amongst us in Carlisle, the Rev George Bramwell Evens, a Methodist Minister, who had been responsible for the building and funding of the Methodist Central Hall in Fisher Street, another focal point in all post war Carlisle lives as a major meeting hall.

Every child of course loved Toy Town, Uncle Mac and Aunty Kathleen. I think Aunty Kathleen might have been a Scottish version, who spoke nicely to Scottish children only, while Uncle Mac was national, uncle to us all. One of my proudest moments in childhood was getting a letter from the BBC, Queen Margaret Drive, Glasgow. I'd entered a competition for a poem on Scottish Children's Hour, presumably under the encouragement of my mother. I didn't win, but I got a silver pencil. I also had a poem published in a Sunday School magazine for children.

The most nerve wrecking, intense, radio listening took place when England was playing Scotland at football. I longed for Scotland to win, my little heart pounding. In my football album, I mainly had Scottish stars, such as Billy Houliston, a cannon ball centre forward who played for Queen of the South, the Dumfries club. I cut their photos out of the newspapers, especially any Pink 'uns I could find, and stuck them in with home-made paste, made out of flour. They started off all soggy and gooey, but after a day or so, they stood up stiff on their album pages, as if they had come to life, become three dimensional.

My dad was interested in football, and had played a lot while in the RAF, but he never took me as a boy to Carlisle United. It wasn't his team, his town, so he had no connection with it or no tradition of going there and probably didn't know where Brunton Park was. Being passionate about your local club runs in families. Football relies on fathers taking sons along while still quite young, so the

A Carlisle United team from 1957
Left to right. Back: Dick Young, (trainer), Forbes, Whitfield, Fletcher, Fairley, Mitton, Hill, Johnston, Waters.
Front row: Kerr, Garvie, Broadis, Atkinson, Bond, Devlin.

baton is handed on.

It was cheap enough in the 1950's to watch Carlisle United, but for a long time I couldn't afford it and rarely went, except on big occasions, which of course were very few. CUFC seemed doomed to be one of nature's Third Division North also ran clubs.

Reg, my best friend, was not a football fan, which was surprising, considering his father - also called Reg Hill - had been a professional and had actually played for Carlisle United, before ending up at 14 MU. None of my other close friends in my teenage years were football fans either, but that didn't stop me being passionate about the game, playing it all the time and following the fortunes of Carlisle United and our local heroes, such as Paddy Waters, Billy Hogan, Geoff Twentyman, Carlisle's bean pole captain and centre half in 1950.

Carlisle also had its own super star in Ivor Broadis, probably the best known person in Carlisle in the 1950's, who had once played for England and had two spells with Carlisle, in the late 40's and again in the late 50's. He was a household name, even to those who didn't follow football. You could tell jokes about him and everyone would

ARSENAL

COLOURS—SHIRTS: RED, WHITE SLEEVES AND COLLARS. KNICKERS: WHITE. STOCKINGS: BLUE,
WHITE RINGS, WHITE TOPS.

Goal
~~Swindin~~
PLATT

2
Right Back
Barnes

3
Left Back
Smith, L.

4
Right Half
Forbes

5
Centre Half
Compton

6
Left Half
Mercer
(Capt.)

7
Outside Right
Cox

8
Inside Right
Logie

9
Centre Forward
Goring

10
Inside Left
Lewis

11
Outside Left
Roper

Referee
Mr. W. R. Rogers
(Birmingham)

Linesmen
Mr. L. C. Howes (Gt. Yarmouth)
Red Flag
Mr. P. H. Straten (Romford)
Yellow Flag

In the event of a draw the replay at Carlisle will take place on the following Thursday.

11
Outside Left
McCue

10
Inside Left
Jackson

9
Centre Forward
~~Lindsay~~
Bellingham

8
Inside Right
Turner

7
Outside Right
Hogan

6
Left Half
Waters

5
Centre Half
Twentyman

4
Right Half
Kinloch

3
Left Back
Coupe

2
Right Back
McIntosh

Goal
McLaren

CARLISLE UNITED

COLOURS—SHIRTS : ROYAL BLUE. KNICKERS : WHITE. STOCKINGS : BLUE AND WHITE.

Arsenal v CUFC, January 1951, in the FA Cup. Carlisle got a goalless draw, which meant the mighty Arsenal had to come to Brunton Park.

get it. Which footballer needs a big sofa? Ivor Broadis! I've a Broad Arse. Ha ha, got you there, chaw.

Professional footballers were of course relatively badly paid in those days, before the maximum £20-a-week wage was abolished, but even so, I was surprised one day to find myself on the C3 bus going from St Ann's to town and sitting beside one of Carlisle's players. Can't remember his name now, but he was living in digs on our estate. A few years later, Stan Bowles, a star of the 1971 team, was also living locally, in a rented semi at Etterby Lea, a fairly modest house, I thought, for such a glamorous player.

Carlisle's greatest achievement in the 1950's was drawing in the third round of the FA Cup with the mighty Arsenal at Highbury in January, 1951, a goal-less draw, though our manager, Bill Shankly, thought Arsenal were lucky. 'I'm disapppointed, we should have won,' he was reported as saying when the final whistle blew. 'I'll give them what for in the dressing room.'

Several thousand had gone down from Carlisle to London for the game, taking with them some Cumberland fox hounds, which were paraded on the pitch before kick-off. But the excitement was nothing compared with the return fixture at Brunton Park with the whole of the city desperate for tickets.

The match was to be held on the Thursday afternoon at two o'clock, there being no floodlights in those days. Everything came to

a standstill, including the local schools. We at the Creighton were to get a half day off, along with the Margaret Sewell, the Grammar and High schools, all of us being quite near Brunton Park. Over at the High School, we heard about one of the younger girls who had petitioned against this half day off, maintaining that it was ridiculous schools being closed for a silly football match. But fortunately her protests were ignored.

The young girl who maintained that it was ridiculous to close schools for a silly football match

On the afternoon itself, Thursday, Jan 11, 1951, Brunton Park was full, with 20,900

55

inside. As so often happens on such occasions, the better, mightier side doesn't make the same mistake twice and underestimate the opposition. Carlisle got beaten 2-0. I've still got my ticket, priced 1/6 to the ground, but not the programme. Perhaps I was not able to afford one.

I've been trying to buy one ever since, as I now have an extensive collective of CUFC memorabilia, including programmes for all the home games for the miracle season of 1974-5 when we were in the First Division. Pre-war CUFC programmes are very hard to find and expensive. Carlisle, being a small club, never printed as many programmes as First Division clubs, which means that a 1930's Carlisle programme is far more expensive than one for Arsenal. So, in one way, we won in the end.

I love looking at my old Carlisle United programmes, not just for the football history but the local shops and businesses now gone, such as Gordon Easton, which was a sports equipment shop in Lowther Street, or William Dand, another sports outfitter, who had shops in English Street and Botchergate. Dand's boasted the 'largest stock of footballs in the county'. I never bought anything there, just pressed my nose to the window, trying to smell the leather, longing to buy a new pair of boots or perhaps a proper leather football.

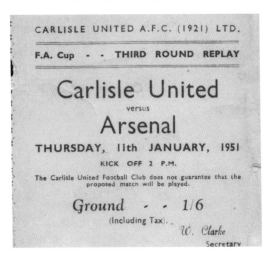

56

Chapter 6

Fun and Games

I did not go as regularly as I would have liked to Brunton Park in the 1950's, as it cost money, but every week-end I still trailed down Warwick Road, trudging all the way, to attend Warwick Road Presbyterian Church. The elders and regular worshippers were pleasant enough, but the sermons were endless and boring, the whole atmosphere cold and depressing.

My father never went to church, even when he was well, although he banned me from playing football or riding a bike on a Sunday, on religious grounds. I always argued against this, pointing out he was not religious. 'Do what I say, not what I do.' Most respectable working class parents, especially Scottish ones, were the same, brought up to revere the Sabbath, even if they were not church goers.

My mother always went to church and forced me and my sisters and brother to attend Sunday School when we were young and then accompany her as we got older to church services as well. At Sunday

Above: Boy Scouts, 17th Carlisle Church of Scotland Troop, 1950. I am in the back row, 4th from left. Reg Hill is 7th left, back row.

School, I was awarded a Lord Wharton Bible, which I still have. To win it, you had to memorise and recite reams of psalms and verses from the Bible. I don't know how I did it, as I am lousy at memorising, can never remember my own children's phone numbers, or why, as it was all so boring.

My mother was not a disciplinarian, never forced us to do things with threats or force, but she would nag on, look pathetic or sad, hoping my better self would make me want me to go to church. Most Sundays I did, to please her.

Warwick Road Presbyterians didn't have a scout troop, so I joined the 17th Church of Scotland Troop in Chapel Street, along with my friend Reg. I loved the scouts, and never missed, unless I was ill. We played boisterous games of British Bulldog, running up and down on the bare floors of the church hall, did tests and exercises, went on scout parades. I eventually became Patrol Leader of the Owl Patrol, what an honour, and yet I never passed any badges, except my tenderfoot badge. We considered ourselves an intellectual troop, at least Reg and I did, making a deliberate point of not being competitive or pot hunting, compared with those other Carlisle troops we met on scout parades, whose patrol leaders had badges covering every part of their uniform, so much so that they could hardly walk, weighed down with all their honours.

We went on week-end meetings and camps to Rattlingate, the local camp for Carlisle's scout troops, out to the west of the City, along the Burgh Road. It appeared to be in the depth of the country and I remember walking back from it after one camp, carrying my kit, and it seemed to take days to reach the City boundary, but in fact it was only a few miles away. Today, it's practically suburbia.

The highlight of the year was the annual proper camp, which lasted at least a week, usually in Scotland, as we were a Church of Scotland troop. One year it was Edinburgh, another time Aberdeen. The food was always awful, burned and tasteless, the tents smelly and uncomfortable and the sleeping bags cold and wet. I was usually wracked with asthma, but still I always enjoyed it. I didn't have a holiday, otherwise.

There was always some older kid in the tent who would show

off his erection, or get you to do the same, or tell dirty stories in the dark, but all the scout leaders were above reproach, genuinely loved teaching and instructing the younger boys. It was only later I heard people making sniggery jokes about scout masters and what they got up to, nudge nudge. Our Skip was always a hero to us, admired by all.

I was once on a train, aged about ten, going to visit my relations in Scotland, on my own, standing in the corridor waiting to go to the lavatory, when I felt this hand going up my short trousers. I didn't understand what was going on at first, but the look in this middle-aged man's eye made me realise something unpleasant might be about to happen, so I ran away, back to my seat, but never told anyone.

In Caird Avenue, there was an older boy, probably aged about 20, and when I was about ten or eleven, he invited me into his house one day and asked me hold his cock. It was huge, hot and rather steaming. I was fascinated by it, rather than revolted. I couldn't work out where it had come from, or whether he was unusual in having such a throbbing monster. He didn't make me toss him off, nor did he do it to himself. It just sort of lay there, then he put it away and went upstairs. Again, I didn't tell anyone about this incident, yet the image stayed in my mind for many years, becoming rather unsettling, more horrible and frightening than it had done at the time.

Amongst the healthiest, most approved of and most enjoyable activities for Carlisle children in the 1950's was the ABC Minors, the cinema show for children held every Saturday morning at the Lonsdale in Warwick Road. I can still sing the song we used to shout out at the tops of our voices.

> We are the boys and girls well known as
> Minors of the ABC
> And every Sa-tur-day we line up to see
> The films we joke and shout about with glee.

I think those are the right words. It went to the tune of the march called 'Blaze Away'.

We got cartoons, little films, and then the big picture which was usually an exciting serial, mostly cowboys and indians, or cops and robbers with lots of chases and escapes, the goodies always winning.

The interior of Lonsdale Cinema.

Before the show, there were announcements and notices and kids whose birthday it was were invited on stage and all got a big cheer, plus a present. You'd often spot the same kids coming up every week to get their birthday present. There were row monitors, older kids who were supposed to help keep the unruly from fighting or the bored and restless from climbing over and under the seats. Some monitors, especially ones slightly older and more mature, wouldn't care about the noise, their arms around and up a girl who was equally advanced, taking advantage of being able to sit in the dark, unseen by adults.

When I was a bit younger, I also used to go and watch silent films, such as Charlie Chaplin films, at a mission hall down Etterby Road, near Caledonian Buildings. They were organised by something called the Rechabites who were passionate tee-totallers and tried to rope children in at an early age, convinced that they would then stay sober for ever. You had to recite their pledge, before the film was shown, agreeing that strong drink was raging, wine a mockery and whomsoever indulged in either would be damned for ever. It was all gibberish to me, but having trotted it out, you saw the films for free.

From a fairly early age, probably about ten or so, I was sent to violin lessons. I don't know how my mother ever afforded it, when we had so little money to spare. I was the only boy on our estate who did such a thing, and I was bit ashamed, as it seemed such a girly, pretentious sort of activity. It was as if she was trying to be socially and culturally something she was not. My mother's father had played the fiddle, and probably never went to lessons, just picked it up, so that was doubtless my mother's motiviation. She had always loved her father, while being a bit scared of her mother. I think she might

Alf Adamson and Donald Scott

have got a special discount from my violin teacher who probably knew about our family circumstances.

I hated the lessons, was useless at it, but liked the teacher, Alf Adamson, well known in musical circles in Carlisle for many years. He ran the Border Square-dance Band, which played folk music all over Carlisle and the Borders, in the style of Jimmy Shand and his Band. He also conducted the Carlisle Light Orchestra who rehearsed in some draughty rooms on Sundays in an old building in Tower Street. I was allowed now and again to go and sit in and listen while they bashed away at Beethoven's Second or Dvorak's New World

Symphony. Now and again, if they were short, I joined the back of the second violins, just pretending to play, moving my bow a few inches above the strings, knowing I was useless. I could never master any of the positions, like third and fifth, my left handing sliding down and getting the wrong notes. If I stayed in the first position, without going up and down, then I was not so bad.

I always put off practising until about half an hour before I was due at my weekly lesson. Mr Adamson lived at Etterby Lea Road, in a pebble-dash semi-detached, and had a daughter at the High School with big breasts called Norma whom, when I got older, I used to ogle, hoping she would come into the room. Even though I was useless, I did develop a liking for classical music, especially Sibelius, which stayed with me for a long time, until I realised I preferred music written for me now, by people like me, not dead music from another age. I must eventually have got reasonable enough on the violin to appear in public - notably at a Scout Concert, run by our troop, the 17th Church of Scotland, in the Chapel Street Hall. I played Haydn's Serenade. I bet it was excruciating, but people clapped politely.

The highlight of my violin career was playing at the Carlisle and District Music Festival. This was a big annual event, which had

Micky Potts, left, and the Gateway Jazz Band.

begun in 1896, held in the Methodist Central Hall in Fisher Street. I was entered in the Under 15 violin category for which only four people had entered. I was fourth. Last, in other words.

While waiting to perform, I watched a boy of my age, Micky Potts, playing the piano, looking smug, satisfied, very middle class, so I thought, hating him because he was so good. In my mind, he was wearing a bow tie, like Little Lord Fontleroy, but I think he was probably just in his Grammar School blazer. I later got to know him quite well, as many people in Carlisle did, through his excellent Gateway Jazz Band. He was a great trumpeter and engaging personality, not at all smug, well loved by all who knew him and died far too young. One thing about a small town, but one big enough to support thriving instituitions, like bands and theatre groups and orchestras, is that certain people become known to all, part of Carlisle folklore, even though you personally have not met them, only seen or heard them or read about them in the local papers. Apart from Micky Potts, there was and is Donald Scott, a brilliant comedian whom I'm sure would have achieved national fame if only he'd started at a different time and in a bigger city.

Other people we all knew, without in this case knowing her real name, included the Woman at the City Picture House. She sat in the box office in her dark red velvet full length gown. It had a hood which she pulled up over her head when walking down the street, floating along like the French Lieutenant's Woman. I often saw her walking up Stanwix Bridges, so she must have lived up there, somewhere. No one seemed to know anything about her, a mystery woman, about whom stories were told, mostly made up. I've recently been told she was called Amy and she died not long ago in her 90's.

The City Picture House was situated where Marks and Spencer now is, one of Carlisle's many picture houses, now gone. At one time, there were nine in all. The Public Hall in Chapel Street was the oldest, opened 1906. The City and the Botchergate Cinema opened during the First World War. The Palace, which was further down Botchergate, on the right, was originally a music hall but became a cinema in 1930. The Lonsdale, Carlisle's poshest cinema, opened in 1931. Then there was the Rex in Caldewgate, the Regal in Denton

Holme and the Stanley in Botchergate, which like the Public Hall in Chapel Street, were flea pits when I was a boy, very basic but cheap. Carlisle's ninth cinema to open, now also gone, was the Argyll in Harraby which opened in 1956.

'Not Many Left' was another Carlisle institution, though we now don't talk about him as much, since he has fallen from grace having been named in a court case. He sold papers at the corner of Bank Street, shouting out the same words in his deep, booming voice, 'Not Many Left' all day long, even when you could see the papers had just arrived and he still had a huge pile.

Another living legend was Lionel Lightfoot, though you had to be one of the more cultured masses to know about him and his achievements. He was the amateur theatre star of the 1950's, either directing or starring in the big Gilbert and Sullivan productions. In real life he was a solicitor. In real life, Alf Adamson, the violinst, did something totally different - delivering tea for Rington's. Donald Scott worked for the Co-op as a painter amongst other things and Micky Potts ran a family textile firm. They all had proper, paid jobs throughout their working life, but just happened to put a huge amount of their energy and time into something else, mostly for no payment, and it was for this they became well known. Famous in their lunch hours about sums it up.

My mother loved the theatre, going most Mondays to Her Majesty's Theatre in Lowther Street when the plays were on, either amateur or professional. The Salisbury Arts were the professional rep company I mostly remember, who seemed for ever to be putting on Black Mischief. They came to Carlisle every season, alternating several plays at a time. They seemed so slick, so talented, so clever - how did they manage to memorise all the parts one week, then move on to something different the following week? Their lives appeared Bohemian, exotic, all of them either handsome or pretty.You would catch glimpses of them at the stage door, a whiff of their French cigarettes, a hint of their London style clothes and smart lives. Were they all sleeping with each other, so we wondered as we got older, having a marvellous, carefree life? In reality, they were probably in scruffy digs down London Road, on very low pay

Her Majesty's Theatre in Lowther Street, now a car park.

and hating each other, bitter and twisted that they hadn't made the West End. I can remember Carroll Levis and his discoveries, Billy Cotton's Band Show and when it was a play, the programme always said 'Cigarettes by Abdulla, Telephone kindly lent by the GPO and Furniture supplied by Messrs Binns'.

Variety shows did still come to Carlisle, on probably number five tours of the smaller cities, and I sometimes did go and see them with Reg or other friends, if just to laugh and mock. There was a woman who did bird noises who had us convulsed at the stupidity of it all, yet how seriously she was taking herself. Or contortionists, jugglers, ventriloquists. 'That's very difficult' older members of the audience would mutter, clapping very politely, while we sat bemused and unappreciative.

I was impressed by Her Majesty's, by its size and grandeur, seating 900 people, by the stalls and boxes and the Gods where we sat, right up in the sky, but I was not aware at the time about its glorious

65

history, how many of the greatest acts and stars of the 19th and 20th centuries had played at Her Majesty's, if only on their way to even bigger, grander theatres in Glasgow or Newcastle. It opened in 1874 and Charlie Chaplin, Laurel and Hardy, Harry Lauder, Noel Coward and others all peformed there. By the end of the 1950's it was coming to the end of its great days. In 1963 it closed. For a time it became a Bingo Hall, finally being demolished in 1979 to become, oh, the sadness of it, a car park.

It was during the period when they were pulling down lots of buildings behind Lowther Street for road reconstruction, including George Street where the school clinic used to be. I went to the clinic once when I had nits and had blue stuff put in my hair. George Street did contain genuine Georgian houses - now it has gone and in its place we have the empty, soulless but grandly named Georgian Way.

If it was happening now, various preservation societies and other bodies might have saved HM Theatre and George Street, but when I was growing up, Carlisle didn't appear to have an active, middle or professional class, apart from Lionel Lightfoot and his theatrical friends. The Council was just allowed to go ahead with things. The quality and the poshos lived well out in the country, and had nothing to do with the City.

Stanwix was where our middle classes lived, and appeared to us to be of superior quality, but most of them spoke much like us, did much the same things, cared no more about preservation or saving Carlisle's heritage than anyone else. It was in the Sixties that action groups got going, too late to do much about the hideous Civic Centre which went up in 1964. In the Seventies, during all the ring road work, they did manage to save places like Spencer Street. They failed to save the Old Lanes, but they did make sure the New Lanes shopping development, when it started opening in 1984, looked from the outside as pleasing as possible without ruining the skyline of the City centre. And it did go on to win various awards.

The Old Lanes were rather run down in my youth, but they did have a nice medieval feeling to them, with ancient shops and businesses, some of them rather subversive, selling communist literature or dodgy rubber goods. They were very handy for dashing down between Lowther Street and the Town Hall to catch a bus home. If I concentrate hard, I can think of the names of most of them - Globe Lane, Grapes Lane, Packhorse, Old Bush, Crown and Anchor, most of them named after ancient coaching inns, fronting on to Scotch Street or Lowther Street, with their stables down the adjoining lane.

The Public Baths in James Street are still with us, in the same building which was opened in 1884, though thankfully they have been smartened up and extended in recent years. I went with the Creighton School each week, and often on Saturdays as well, if I had the money. Being small and weedy and asthmatic, I wasn't much good at swimming, and usually stood around the dressing room for a lot of the time, shivering with the cold. I was never in a swimming club, like the Dolphins or the Border City. They entailed a member-ship fee, which I could not raise, and regular attendance and practice, but what put me off was the look of the sadists who seemed to run these clubs, shouting at kids in the water, poking them with long sticks, making them do length after length.

Looking back, I don't know why I went so often. But it was what one did at a time of relatively few attractions for children. If you were in a little gang, someone would say let's go swimming. In the summer we would go to the Eden, down by Caledonian Buildings, but mostly it meant the Baths. You went along with what the gang did, otherwise you were on your own. No one wanted to be on their own. If you did fall out with your gang, and they went off and did exciting things without you, you were distraught, even when you knew that all they were doing was just hanging around in the street or mucking around in the Buildings, till a watchman chased them. The Buildings were the new council houses going up behind the lotties, in Briar Bank, in what is now known as Belah.

The main pleasure of going swimming was what happened after-wards - going round the shops, begging for a penny bag of broken biscuits. Our favourite places were Liptons and the Home and Colonial, grocery shops quite near each other at the end of the Viaduct and Scotch Street, near the present Woolworths. There were one or two nice smiley friendly women in each shop, probably only teenagers, but they seemed grown up to us, who if you smiled nicely and looked appealing, they would fill a bag with really good biscuits, hardly any of them broken. If you got one of the mean, nasty ones, you had wasted a penny on a bag of dust.

My favourite sweetshop was Stuart's or perhaps it was Stewart's which was on Scotch Street, opposite Chapel Street, down which most kids from the locals schools would trail, before and after school. We desired anything with sherbert, which fizzed in your mouth or liquorice laces. With age and sophistication, say around twelve or thirteen, I got a passion for Palm Toffee. My mother loved bars of Cadbury's milk chocolate, especially when drinking a cup of tea, and she would often spare me a square, which was kind.

I haven't eaten sweets since I was child. I never buy them, not even chocolates, and refuse them when offered. I hate the taste of all of them. Yet as a child I dreamt about them and my fantasy was to be let loose alone in a sweetshop. I find it bizarre when so called grown-ups stuff their faces with sweets, though on the whole, it seems to be women who retain a sweet tooth through life, rather than men. They say it comes back in old age, especially a longing for ice cream. But then, in the end, everything from your early life is likely to come back in some form.

Chapter Seven

Work and Play

I started work in 1950 when I was fourteen. Not down the mines, pulling donkeys, or naked up the chimney swallowing soot, but as a paper boy. It seemed to me just as knackering and exhausting as any of the 19th century sweated labour jobs which children did. I got taken on by Clark's, our local shop, in Kingmoor Road, opposite the end of Belah Road. To get there each morning, I went from our house in Caird Avenue up Belah Road, so I was exhausted even before I'd started delivering the rotten papers.

It was a family shop, run by Mr and Mrs Clark, which seemed always busy, as it served the whole of the St Ann's estate, though later there was also a little Co-op further along the road. Clark's did everything - newspapers, sweets, bread, groceries. I never knew Mr Clark's first name, or his wife's, but their children, who eventually helped in the shop as well, included Peter, who was about my age, and Marion who was blond and went to the High School. They also had at least two full-time female assistants. It must have been a pretty

Above: Creighton School trip to France, me on right, 1951.

Clark's as it is today.

thriving business, but Mr Clark always seemed tired and miserable, especially first thing in the morning, glaring at any paper boys who were late. There was great competition to work there, so no one wanted to upset him and lose their precious job.

We had to be there at six o'clock each morning, which meant that most of the year it was still dark, which made it even more hellish to get up in time. I moaned and groaned every morning and often my mother had to force me out of bed, knowing how much the job mattered to me. When I was ill with asthma, which often happened, and I couldn't walk, far less carry the huge paper bag, my mother would then waken the twins, Marion and Annabelle, and make them get up and take my place, as Mr Clark could not be let down. I'd then have to pay them for doing my round, which always annoyed me.

I delivered papers for at least four years. Afterwards, when I'd eventually given up, my mother used to tell me that I was never as bright and good tempered in the mornings as in those years when I did the papers. That was never my memory, but she later insisted on telling my wife this, who still trots out this idiotic remark every morning around 8.30 when I'm still unable to open my eyes and face the day.

In the summer and autumn there was a certain charm to it, once I'd got myself up and on my way walking alone on a bright new dawn before the rest of the world had wakened up. The autumn was especially good. Along with a couple of other boys, one keeping watch, we'd nick apples from a nursery at the end of Belah Road, then munch our way on our rounds.

My round included my own street, Caird Avenue, and the surrounding streets, Deer Park Grove, Fraser Grove, Hallaway and Belah Road. I can still roughly remember which houses got a News Chron, a Daily Herald, Daily Sketch, Daily Mirror and an Express. I don't recall anyone getting a Times or a Guardian, but there might have been one Telegraph at the posh end of Caird Avenue, one of those who had changed their door knocker to a bell, a sure sign of social mobility.

Best of all was Christmas. For weeks beforehand, I was unusually cheerful and charming, always on time, keeping in with even the grumpy, bad tempered houses. I depended on a good tip from every household to keep me going for the following year. I soon found out that it was the impoverished, scruffier houses with overgrown gardens and half naked kids running around, who gave the best tips. The Telegraph house, and similar with well kept gardens, were often the meanest. It helped that they all knew me, and my family, but I didn't realise for many years that I got such good tips not because of my charm and efficiency but because they were taking pity on me. I still meet people who say oh, we felt so sorry for you, poor wee boy, carrying that big load, wheezing away, with your father an invalid and all.

Life has now come full cycle. At Loweswater, every Saturday I go to Lorton and pick up the papers and deliver them to our Loweswater neighbours, part of the local pool system, as our nearest town, Cockermouth, is seven miles away. The only difference today is that I drive when doing the papers - in my old Jaguar.

In the 1950's, my paper round money was absolutely vital to me as it provided the only earned income coming into the house. Not that I gave any of it to my mother. It all went into my Raleigh Lenton Sports. Oh, the joy of having one's own bike, freedom at last. I got it from TP Bells in Abbey Street, paying up 13/11 per week on the never-never. That sum has clearly stayed in my mind, yet I can't remember what I was paid for the paper round. Perhaps ten shillings a week at first, hence I needed tips, but it went up, very slowly, each year on your birthday.

TP Bells, even then, was a very old fashioned shop run by brothers, one very small and owl-like who never spoke. I'd go there each Saturday, after I got paid, to hand over my weekly money and get my card signed. My bike was green and had three-speed Sturmey Archer gears and racing handlebars, the most desirable model on the planet, lusted after by all boys.

I was so proud that I'd bought it all my myself. Until I started the paper round, I never had any money. I got no pocket money, and never expected it, as I knew my mother had nothing to spare. All I relied on, till I got the paper job, was a half crown from visiting relations, or perhaps money from empty pop bottles. If you collected the right ones, took them back to the right shop, you got a penny on each. Reg and I, after a children's sports day at 14 MU held on their site near Rockcliffe, collected up about a dozen empty bottles each and carted them all the way to Clark's, which was several miles away. When we eventually got there, staggering in the heat, Mr Clark refused to take them, saying they had not been bought at his shop. How we hated him.

Once I'd got my bike, I could cycle out to Rockcliffe when I felt like it, or into town. I went to school on the bike, whizzing down Stanwix Bank, terrifying myself by going too fast. In the winter, my legs and face would be frozen by the time I'd got to school.

My bike also enabled me to play football further afield, instead of just in the lotties behind Caird Avenue. Thanks to Stan Wharton, I joined Kingstown Rovers in the Carlisle and District Under 15 Christian Welfare League. Stan was our milkman, but he also ran a boys football team as a hobby. Later on, he moved into motor cars and had a garage and a concession for one of the first of the Japanese cars or at least some foreign make. I think it was the same Stan Wharton, or his son. Hmm. I've just looked for his name in the Carlisle phonebook, but can't find it. Anyway, I was very grateful to him for organising a boys football team.

I was able to cycle to Kingstown for home games, on our own pitch, which was off California Road, such a romantic name for an empty dusty road which led nowhere. Our strip was red and white chequered squares, a bit like the old Blackburn Rovers strip, except they played in blue. We changed in a little mission hall with stained glass windows. When we played away, at places right across the City, we often got stripped off at the side of the pitch, which meant if it rained, you had to put on wet clothes.

I discovered pitches and parks in far remote districts of Carlisle which I never knew about. I was astounded by a park somewhere in Denton Holme which had a proper little grandstand, goal posts and nets. We also played out in the country, at places like Thursby and Wetheral, where great beefy farm boys would thump us 10-0.

I wasn't very good, but ever so keen and eager. I had a good football brain, so I liked to think, an inside forward able to spot the killer pass and thread it through. The trouble was I didn't have the strength. A football in those days, with brown leather panels and a rubber bladder inside, weighed about a ton when it got wet, as it retained all the moisture, so it was like trying to kick a lead balloon. My killer passes often travelled only a few yards, very slowly, and were easily cut off.

At home, I played in the street, under the lampposts when it was dark. There were so few cars, that even an eleven-a-side game, running the length of Caird Avenue, would hardly get interrupted by traffic.

I practised against our back wall for hours with a tennis ball, making myself return the ball with either foot. I thought if I'm going to become a professional, as I'd told the Creighton headmaster, I'd need to be two footed. I even took dead balls, such as corners and free kicks, with my left foot, i.e. my wrong foot. Now that is hard. Beckham, for all his skills, always takes free kicks with his best foot. When you are running, in full flow, then it is not so hard for a half decent player to use his so called weaker foot, if the pass requires it. But with a stationary ball, and time to think and worry, even the best players will decide to use their best foot.

Despite my passion for football, and by the age of fourteen and fifteen playing every week in a proper little team, at school I still got myself excused games on health grounds. My asthma was still there, but when it came to football, I'd learned to force myself through the pain barrier. If I could keep going, somehow, the excitement of the game would help me, if only to forget my wheezing. I'm always interested today in watching Paul Scholes or Matt Jansen - who of course comes from Carlisle - knowing they had bad asthma as boys. I think I can tell by the hunch of their shoulders, the way they stand to recover their breath, that for a moment they are worried a wheeze might be coming on.

After a year or so of doing the morning papers, I took on an evening round as well which was much lighter and easier as not many got the Cumberland Evening News delivered, but it meant going further afield as I did Briar Bank as well.

I then added another job. I became Clark's messenger boy. This was mainly a Saturday job, delivering groceries, for which I used a huge old fashioned bike, with a massive basket in front, very heavy and clumsy, hard to control when full. The beginning of each round was down hill, when the load was heaviest, so that was a help.

I mostly delivered bread, sliced loaves wrapped in grease-proof paper, which I think were a relatively new invention, hence the best thing since sliced bread. They were baked by Robertsons and delivered still hot to Clark's, then I delivered them to customers. If I had overloaded the bike, some flew off and would split and I would have to gather up the slices from the street, wipe off the dirt, then shove them back in the package, hoping customers wouldn't notice.

Saturday was the hardest day, when I also took people their weekly groceries, packed in a box by Mr or Mrs Clark. Customers left their orders during the week and would check the items off before I was allowed to leave, just in case there was anything missing. I couldn't understand why people had groceries delivered, it seemed so lazy, but it was mainly to households where wives were out working during the week. They would often come to their back doors on Saturday morning still in their nightdresses and slippers which as I got older, used to send my imagination soaring, especially when they said step in Hunter, I might have something for you . . . I would stand in the kitchen, waiting for them to find their purse and give me a tip. That was all I ever got, though I lived in hope. At school, we heard stories about young housewives seducing young boys, which I didn't believe, why would any proper grown up woman want to go to bed with an awkward, inexperienced fifteen year old. The fantasy of having sex with an older woman was very alluring, if a bit scary. (Years later, I made great play with this in my first book, later a film, Here we Go Round the Mulberry Bush.)

I was therefore quite well off, having two jobs, though a bike was quite expensive to run, as tyres had to be replaced, things mended, but I managed to save enough to go on a cycling holiday with my friend Reg. We each went on our bikes to Glasgow, weighed down with pannier bags, carrying all our belongings. We went on the main road, the A74, which even in those days, was a nightmare, with lorries and buses rattling along, and no dual carriageway. We stayed with my relations in Glasgow, Uncle Jim and Aunt Linda, my Bohemian, literary relations, so I liked to think, and visited places like Rothesay and Loch Lomond.

In 1952, aged fifteen, I went to France, with the Creighton School. It was an educational trip, mainly aimed at those doing French O Levels. I don't know how my mother afforded it, for I certainly didn't pay for it, or whether the school helped in any way. I realised it was a big sacrifice for my mother, that I was getting special treatment, something Marion, Annabelle and Johnny didn't get. Neither of my parents had ever been abroad in their lives, though my father boasted that he had once flown in a plane, when in the RAF, going right across the English Channel and back, though without landing in France.

We stayed at the railway hotel in Abbeville. The first smells and tastes and sights of France were startling, so different and exotic in every way. Even the plumbing was different, and the little fat bottles of orange juice, the fat tyres they had on their bikes, the shoes and clothes people wore, the smell of Gauloises and of course the food, which I had never come across before. None of it had ever appeared in the boxes of groceries I delivered from Clarks, which was mainly sliced bread, tinned beans, H P Sauce and custard powder.

The trip included a stay in Paris, where we did the Eiffel Tower, Notre Dame and the usual sites. In Paris, I fell ill with asthma and had to stay in bed. One of the teachers stayed behind in the hotel with me, which was very kind, and must have ruined his trip to Paris.

There were about a dozen of us, boys from my year at the Creighton, including three teachers. Although the object was to help our French, I can't remember speaking French to any French people, except asking for drinks in bars. I brought home a model of the Eifel Tower in a snow storm for my mother and a miniature bottle of three star cognac for my father, both of which went straight into our cocktail cabinet, souvenirs of a foreign trip but also to impress any neighours. Go on Hunter, speak some French to Mrs Forsyth, so my mother would say when our neighbour from across the street popped in.

I did think I was pretty good at French, compared with most people in my class at the Creighton, but that turned out to be another fantasy.

Chapter Eight

With the Brain Boxes at Last

I sat my General Certificate of Education O Levels at the Creighton School in 1952. I did nine subjects - English Lang, Eng Lit, French, History, Geography, Maths, General Science, RE and Technical Drawing. I passed seven and failed two. I never expected to get through Tech Drawing, as I was so useless at it, but I was appalled and ashamed to fail French, after that expensive trip to France, after saying how much I liked it. I'm not sure if anyone else in my class got through or not, which would indicate the teaching was at fault, but that's beside the point. I should still have passed.

At the time, I blamed Reg. The night before the French exam, he had arrived at my house with a couple of other Grammar School boys and encouraged me to come out. I said I had some last minute swotting to do, but he persuaded me.

I think four if not five others in my year also got seven O Levels, which was pretty good, for so called Grammar School failures at a

Carlisle Grammar School Sixth Form, 1953, plus staff. I am standing in the front row, fourth from left. At the very back from the left are Mike Thornhill and Reg Hill.

supposedly second division school. In fact we did as well as the Grammar School. I've just looked up on microfiche at the Reference Library the Cumberland News for August 21, 1954, and I see that the Grammar School had only one boy who got eight passes - my friend Ian Johnson, while Reg Hill and Brian Donaldson got seven, the same as me, and the rest mainly got five or so passes.

And then a strange thing happened. I found myself at the Grammar School.

I say strange because I have no idea how it happened. I have no memory of it being discussed beforehand, or even of it being mentioned as a possibility. I didn't have an interview with anyone at the Grammar, which I'd had to get into the Creighton, nor did my parents request it. To the best of my knowledge there was no system at the time of Creighton boys going on to the Grammar after O Levels. There should have been, in a fair and ideal world, and perhaps that was one of the original intentions after the 1944 Education Act when the Eleven Plus came in, to give people a second chance at sixteen, but I'd never heard of it happening. And I'm sure I would have been aware if anyone in the year ahead of me at the Creighton had gone on to the Grammar. After me, it certainly did happen because I can remember old Creightonians who followed a year later.

I can't believe it was activated by the Grammar School. Hard to imagine someone there waking up one day and saying isn't it about time we gave some of those lesser human beings at that school along the road, now what's its name, another chance in life. In the records of the Carlisle Education Department there must be an explanation. So I have to give thanks to either the Creighton teachers or someone at the education department. And yet, even though it came as a surprise, I can't remember making alternate plans, such as applying to Laings to be an apprentice draughtsman, which I wouldn't have got anyway, or looking for a job at 14 MU. In my mind, which is not of course totally reliable, I just woke up one day and there I was, walking through the ancient front doors of Carlisle Grammar School. An honour in itself, as I quickly discovered. Only sixth formers and staff could use that front door. The rest of the school used another entrance.

The fact that I went straight into the Sixth was also remarkable, because the Grammar had a Fifth Form Remove in which people re-sat a year, if they were not thought quite up to the Sixth or did not have enough O Levels. But I went straight into 6B Modern - which stood for Lower Sixth, the modern bit indicating I was taking Arts subjects. There was also a Science Sixth and a Classics Sixth, though by the 1960's the Classics Sixth was small and they came in with us on the Arts side.

Two other boys came from the Creighton with me into the Lower Sixth - Brian Cooke and Alastair McFadden - and we were to take the same three subjects at A level, English, History and Geography. We were then informed that in order to have a chance of getting into a decent univerisity we would have to have Latin at O level. That was the system in the 1950's and it didn't just apply to Oxbridge but most other universities. I also discovered that I had to re-sit French, as I needed to have passed that at O level as well.

For my French re-sit, I joined the Remove's French class. That wasn't too daunting. After all, I'd had five years of learning French at the Creighton, in theory. But Latin was going to be a problem. How could me and Brian and Alastair hope to do that from scratch, never having had a Latin lesson in our lives, while still fitting in our Sixth Form A level timetable in English, History and Geography?

I wonder if it would have happened now, if any present day teachers, over worked and over stressed as we know they undoubtedly are, would have agreed to do what Mr Hodges did? He was a Latin master, small, mole-like with a moustache, who bustled about with piles of books under his arms. He didn't know us, was unaware of our personal capabilities, but must have realised our grounding in languages, coming from a sec tech. school, wouldn't be exactly top class.

Mr Hodges gave up his free periods in order to take the three of us, on our own, at times which fitted in with our other subjects, and started to teach us Latin from scratch. We met in this funny little attic room at the top of the building, all of us hunched round a little desk. At first, I had no idea what the hell was going on, it was all gibberish. Once we'd roughly got the hang of the basic grammar, he decided that we would concentrate on the set text which was Tacitus and formed a large part of the O level mark. He reckoned if we could memorise enough of it, parrot fashion, as opposed to being able to understand it, word for word, we would be able to translate into English and scrape through the exam.

Mr Hodges - I can't remember his first name, if I ever knew it,- was brilliant, but I have to say some of the other Grammar School masters were a bit a superior and condescending towards us, at least that was how I felt. It was understandable. We had come from a poorer school but most of all, they didn't know us. They had been teaching all the other boys in our class for five years, seen them growing up, knew their talents and potential, and also had their favourites, the ones they liked.

I found Adrian Barnes, the head of English, distant and languid, rather sneering about my work, or so I thought, but Reg and the others said that was his style, he was an Oxford intellectual, superior, but also very laid back, and they all admired him and thought him very clever. Gerry Lightfoot, the other English master, who was not rated quite as highly by Reg and the others, was always kind and helpful and considerate towards me. He gave me my first Alpha for an English essay, so naturally I thought he was an excellent teacher.

Socially, with the other sixth formers, I had no problems at all, because I was also already in Reg's gang, having been his chum since we were four. Over the years, despite being at the Creighton, I had got to know through Reg the other main personalities of his Grammar School year, some of whom had been at Stanwix with me anyway, such as Ian Johnson who lived in Stanwix and whose father was manager of Martin's Bank in Stanwix. The brain box was Dickie Wilson, the boy wonder, brilliant at all languages, who lived up towards Harraby, very untidy, rather eccentric, but so clever he had been moved a year ahead and was already tipped for an Oxbridge scholarship. He was very unassuming, not at all pretensious, with an ordinary background and family. They lived in a semi near Harraby but I think his father had a fairly ordinary, white collar job. Mike Thornhill was the first clearly middle class boy I ever knew. His dad was the Co-op dentist, which today I would hardly rate as a top profession, not compared with say a barrister, but it seemed to me the height of posh. Mike went fishing for salmon in his big waders, was tall and aristocratic looking and when he got to seventeen, he had access to his father's car. He had been at the Grammar School's prep department, not a local state primary. This surprised me, but then I had never really realised, till I got there, that the Grammar School had been in effect an independent, fee paying public schoool, until the 1944 Act, and it remained for some years a member of the Headmasters' Conference. First mention of the school was in 1186, when it was the cathedral school, which makes it older than Eton (founded 1440) or Winchester (1382). It had moved from the cathedral precincts in 1883 into its new premises.

The main building seemed very public school-ish to me, with its Gothic style imposing entrance and ancient tiled hall, compared with the brutally modern, brick built Creighton. All the masters did wear gowns and there was a feeling of intellectual rigour. The headmaster was V J Dunstan, a classics scholar, who seemed not quite of this world. He floated around, in a dream, often followed by his wife,

Carlisle Grammar School, now Trinity.

81

telling him things, who seemed equally weird.

Our form master was Buff Scott, another unusual character who had been at the school for decades. I don't know why he was called Buff. He looked a bit like that officer in Dad's Army and often wore plus fours. He tended to huff and puff a lot and I was surprised to find he was in charge of the school's boy scout troop. He didn't seem macho or hearty enough to be a scout leader. He died while I was at the Grammar School, and, as members of his form, we had to go to his funeral. At the graveside, at Carlisle cemetery, some one pushed me and I accidentally fell in the hole, but I was pulled out, just in time before the coffin arrived.

The Deputy Head was Mr Banks who was in charge of discipline. You went to Mr Banks to get whacked. He was big and bald and had one time been a professional goalkeeper, so I was told. He taught Geography, but not very well. All he did was read out stuff at dictation speed from his ancient notes and we had to write it down. No discussions, no enthusiasm, no spark. I couldn't believe it. Even at the Creighton, no teacher had done that.

I was also surprised by the treatment of Mr Done, the science teacher. He was small, thin, weedy, balding, nervous looking, but was said to have been a brilliant scholar. While I was at the Grammar Shool, it was decided that the Arts Sixth should not be cut off completely from science and we should take an O level in general science, which was mainly about the history of science. It turned out to be quite interesting, except that it was taken by Mr Done who was never given a chance.

He took us in the Library where we all sat round a big table and made his life hell. The table would move for no apparent reason, which we said must be spiritualism, swearing none of us had touched it. He would bend down, to see whose knees were moving the table, and of course we would then all move the table together, so that he was trapped underneath, unable to get out. I followed every one else at playing him up, but felt sorry for him. We would deliberately pronounce famous scientists the wrong way, such as Copper Knickers for Copernicus, which would make everyone else snigger. Mr Done, though, was the only teacher anyone ever took liberties with.

Mr Morlin arrived to take History, and he was quite good, and we all loved it when he was discovered to be going out with a teacher from the High School, whom he eventually married. There was one youngish teacher who was a keen member of the local light opera society and in a Gilbert and Sullivan production, directed no doubt by Lionel Lightfoot, we all went to HM Theatre for the last night where traditionally bouquets of flowers were presented on stage to the leading actors and actresses. We handed up a cabbage, beautifully wrapped, so he didn't know what it was till he had opened it, on stage, in full view of the whole audience. How we howled. We thought we had been ever so witty, but on Monday he was clearly hurt and upset by what we'd done. I think he left not long afterwards.

As sixth formers, we considered ourselves intellectuals, a cut above the rest of the school. As well as going to the theatre, we did our own little play readings in a hall at Stanwix and were all into classical music. I went to the Edinburgh Festival one summer with Reg, staying with some relations of Brian Donaldson, who was in our class. We saw Richard Burton in some Shakespeare play and Menuhin and Isaac Stern playing the violin. I also went to the Proms while in the Sixth Form, hitch hiking down to London and queuing up outside the Albert Hall for tickets. Reg was going to go with me, but something happened and he didn't. I went alone, staying in a youth hostel, going to a Prom concert every evening. Looking back, I now can't believe I did it. Doesn't sound like me at all, preferring symphonies and violin concertos to popular music, but that was me aged 17-18 in the early 1950's. One reason was pretension, trying to be cultured and artistic. The other reason was that popular music at the time was awful, silly novelty songs or sloppy ballads sung in phoney mid-Atlantic accents, aimed at shop girls not intellectual sixth formers.

There was a school magazine, the Carliol, the official mag, run by a master and full of boring poems, twee little stories and sports results. There was also the Sixth Form Debating Society Magazine, an unofficial, semi-underground publication, mainly written by Reg. It didn't have much to do with the Debating Society at all, but Reg and others had found out that as it was deemed part of it, and therefore respectable, they could use the school's duplicating machine and paper to print it.

I thought it was absolutely brilliant, so clever and witty. It was a precursor of Private Eye, in that its purpose was satirical, with drawings and stories, poking fun at the school and Carlisle people and institutions. At the Creighton, we had no such publication, no outlet for such writing, though we did have a concert for which we wrote witty words about the teachers, so we thought.

I never wrote a word for the Deb Soc Mag, as far as I can remember. I believed I couldn't possibly compete, ever be as clever and original as Reggie.

Despite doing A levels, considering myself a full and proper member of the Sixth Form, I still felt slightly second class, not one of the leaders, not quite knowing how the system worked, still a bit of an interloper.

But at the end of the year, I had begun to catch up. I passed my French re-sit and, more amazingly, all three of us from the Creighton got through our O level Latin, after only nine months. So thanks a lot, CGS. And especially Mr Hodges.

Chapter Nine

Wine, Women and Song

From the moment I arrived at the Grammar, I decided to play Games, which meant of course rugby. I had continued to be excused at the Creighton on account of my asthma, right to the end, despite playing football every week-end. It seemed false while still at the Creighton to suddenly announce I'd had a miracle cure, as they all knew how I used to be when I was younger and forced to play. But at the Grammar, I wasn't known. I was a new person, creating a new life. They were not aware nor cared about what had gone before.

I saw it as part of my integration, being accepted into the culture of the school. There were of course a handful of people at the Grammar, as at the Creighton, who were naturally good at all sports, such as Spud Carruthers, but there were also people in the First XV

Above: Carlisle Grammar School hockey team, 1954, about to play the girls of the High School and score, or so we hoped. I am at the front second from right. Reg Hill is at the very back. At the back, are Lawrence Fisher, Fred Farrell, Mike Thornhill, Bobby Leslie. Front left is Brian Cooke, front right is Ian Johnson

85

who didn't have much skill but happened to be big and strong and keen, such as Reg and Mike Thornhill, both of them well over six feet. Schoolmasters always want big lads in their team.

Being small and weedy and not very fast, I decided I had to make myself a good tackler. I realised that even the titchiest kid, if he caught a giant round the legs, and hung on, the giant couldn't move much, far less run. I also realised that on such an impact, with both the giant and the titch falling, the chances were that the giant would hurt as much if not more, because of his greater weight. So I turned myself into a demon tackler, throwing myself at players, hanging on for dear life.

By the second year Sixth, I did get into the First XV. Oh the glory and the status, seeing my name on the team sheet. I never made it as a prefect, though I think eventually I was created a sub prefect, for I have a vague memory of being allowed into the sanctum of the prefects' room. Such things mattered so much at the time, but now I'm not even sure.

Being in the First XV, that is very clear in my mind. We went away in a school coach on Saturdays to places like Whitehaven, Workington and Cockermouth to play against their grammar schools - and usually got thumped. We also played St Bees, West Cumbria's local public school, who beat us as well. Our longest trip was to Newcastle to play the Royal Grammar School, but only their Second XV who also hammered us. It was a bit like being in the Scouts with Reg. The ethos was not about cups and glory, but taking part and enjoying it. Singing on the coach on the way home, trying to smuggle on bottles of beer, that was the best part of playing rugby.

The highlight of my rugby career was one New Year's Day, by which time I had become a member of the school's First XV. I was contacted by Carlisle Rugby Union Club, the city's main rugby club. They were a man short, desperate for anyone they could find, trying to raise a team for a seven-a-side competition at Galashiels. I think they were only sending their second string, but it was still a fairly important event in the local rugby calendar.

There were people in the Border teams we played against who were outstanding, so fast and clever, who left us standing. It was also incredibly cold. I got frozen, just waiting for a pass, or waiting to tackle someone. In schoolboy teams, it was usually pretty clear who was the lump, who might look frightening in the flesh, warming up, but you could soon see he was over-weight, uncoordinated, clumsy and slow, and relatively easily brought down. It didn't work this time as I couldn't catch them.

I became less interested in rugby after that, realising I wasn't any good, could never improve, and that it was more than enough to represent the school. I decided to concentrate more on the other things in life associated with rugby, such as drinking and chasing women.

I started going to pubs about the age of sixteen or seventeen, forcing myself to down half a pint of mild and bitter. Reg and I couldn't go to any local pub, like the Redfern, as we would be spotted by neighbours and our ages known, so we used to go to the Near Boot Inn, right down Brampton Road, near Tarraby, where we would meet Mike and Ian, both of whom lived in Stanwix.

I didn't like the taste of State Management beer, though experts boasted about its quality and good value. It was too bitter for me, but I forced it down, knowing it was stupid to drink stuff I didn't like, purely for the sake of appearing grown-up and manly. The theory was that I would acquire a taste for it. That's what people said would eventually happen. I just had to look around at all the blokes in the pubs, pouring it down, pint after pint, no bother. It had worked for them.

All the pubs we went to seemed cheerless, drab and dreary, though the Near Boot did have a bowling green at the back, as many did, so you could sit out when the weather was fine. But inside, they were purely drinking shops, not places of pleasure or fun. I had so little money anyway, that I had to stick to half a pint of the cheapest beer, and spin it out for an evening.

That of course had been the whole ethos of Carlisle's State Management scheme - to keep control of local drinking, stop it being too much fun. We all knew that Carlisle's pubs were special, unique in England, so that was something to be proud of. The scheme had begun during the First World War when massive munitions works were created at Gretna. On Saturday evenings, up to 5000 workers, most of them Irish navvies, came into Carlisle for the sole purpose of getting pissed out of their heads. They would pile off the train at the Citadel Station, straight into the nearest pubs where the landlords would already have lined up 500 glasses of whisky on the counters. Very often they would have only a short drinking time, depending on the trains and their shift work, so they had to get a lot down in the shortest time. The result was bedlam in the pubs, then chaos in the streets as drunks fought each other, wrecking the town. 'Drunkenness amongst munition workers,' said Lloyd George, Minister of Munitions, 'was doing more damage in the War than all the German submarines put together.'

The solution was to nationalise all the pubs and hotels in Carlisle and District, an unusual move for a so called capitalist country, well ahead of the communists taking charge in Russia. Only a handful of licensed places stayed in private hands, such as the Crown and Mitre, Carlisle's poshest hotel, patronised by the quality, where navvies would not have gone anyway. Grocers lost their licences, no longer able to sell beer and spirits. Four breweries were bought - three being closed with just one remaining, the Old Brewery in Caldewgate. Half the pubs were closed and drinking hours in the ones retained were severely restricted.

Even in the early 1950's, when I started drinking in Carlisle pubs, I was aware of the limited drinking time, having to hang around on Sundays for pubs to open at seven o'clock in the evening. If you wanted to buy beer or spirits to take away, perhaps drink at home, you could only do so at a pub or a hotel, at its so called off-licence department, which was a joke. Usually it was just a hole in the wall, with no display or

proper counter. You had to bang on a trap door on the wall for service, wait and wait, only to be told it was closed. The State Management's own brewery produced its own brand of beers and whiskies. On the occasions I did move on to a half and half, as they call it in Scotland - a half a beer with a small Scotch - I realised that State Management whisky, Border Blend, was relatively cheap, as were the beers, compared with

elsewhere in Cumbria or in England as a whole.

But I wasn't aware, though, at the time, that the State Management's architecture was so interesting, though I often wondered at the weirdness of that pub at the end of Warwick Road, the Crescent, with its Spanish style balconies, green tiles, arched windows. Was it, now I think about it, a complicated visual/verbal pun, built on the symbol of the Moorish, Arabic crescent? In the 1930's, apparently, the State Management had built or re-designed many of their pubs under their own architect Harry Redfern, giving them a distinctive style, such as the Malt Shovel and the Apple Tree. Redfern had been a well known architect in his day, having worked on several Oxbridge colleges. His name lives on in the Redfern pub at St Ann's Hill, where my father used to drink, built and named in Redfern's honour.

The State Management scheme was part of my youth and growing up, as it was for all Carlisle people. My brother Johnny, when he left Kingstown school at fifteen and started work, was for several years an electrician with the State Management.

All Carlisle's pubs were state managed until 1971 when the scheme was de-nationalised, but its heritage remains in the architecture and also in various displays in the museum at Tullie House. If only I'd known when I started my drinking life that I was drinking social history, or how the Redfern pub had got its name.

The first Carlisle girl I remember fancying was called Jennie Hogg. I was in the Scouts and she was in the Girl Guides. I don't think I ever took her out, though I might have walked behind her, admiring from afar. To get to know girls properly you had to pick them up at dances, ask if you could walk them home, then take it from there, which was usually not very far.

Local dances or hops were held in church halls or village halls, sometimes with three-piece live bands but often with just a wind-up gramophone on the stage. People danced a valeta - whatever that was, dashing white sergeants, perhaps even a dinkie two step, or am I making that up. The older fashioned, church based dance halls still had a lot of Scottish formation dances, where you lined up, did various stupid movements, but never got to get a girl in your arms, one to one. You tried to steer clear of those.

To get close to a girl, physically, you had to learn to do the quick step which the fast set always preferred. Once you had mastered it, you could, with a bit of cheek, making the most of a twirl, get your leg between a girl's legs. That way you could feel the shape of her body, if not much else.

Girls often wore stiff petticoats, which had been soaked in starch or icing sugar or something, which made them stick out, and therefore made it harder to get close, though if you twirled them hard enough, the skirts often blew out so you could catch a glimpse of white thigh.

The vital dance was the slow waltz at the end of the dance when the lights dimmed and you might manage to get your arms round her, perhaps even feel her breasts against your chest, if you were lucky. Getting an erection was awkward and embarrassing and there were innocent girls who really did think you had a pen in your pocket. There were others, more worldly, who were cock teasers, who knew what they were doing, but you also knew that that was as far as it would ever get, this being the 1950's.

If they agreed to be taken home, you often found they had a friend, usually less pretty, not to say ugly, whom you had to take home as well, so you got nowhere. If she was on her own, you might get a quick kiss on the doorstep, and that was that, excitement over, then you had to find your way home from some far flung housing estate on the other side of Carlisle and it would take hours to reach the Town Hall and get a C3 or C4 back to St Ann's.

Reg was not much of a dancer so I usually went to dances on my own or with other boys, to the Miles McInnes Hall in Stanwix or to the Wigton Road Methodists. I often went out into the country, such as Wetheral, hoping the girls would be easier there, but they weren't. Eventually, I started to go to the Crown and Mitre, when I got a bit older, and could afford it, such as Christmas time when I was getting good tips from delivering the papers and the groceries at Clark's, which I kept on doing till I was eighteen. I never had any luck at the Crown and Mitre which was for slightly older people. There were often a few county types there, gentleman farmers, so they thought, who stood on the edge of the dance floor, jangling their keys, showing they had access to a car, if only their father's, who got all the girls. Some of them were at St Bees, and looked more affluent, more mature, more sophisticated with better accents. I hated them.

I did try the Cameo in Botchergate, but that was rougher and more frightening. I never went to Bonds which was in Fisher Street and became popular with younger dancers a bit after my time. My sister Annabelle went there and so did my brother Johnny - and it was there he met his wife Marjorie.

I never had much luck with so called lower class girls, from backgrounds the same as mine, who perhaps were working in offices or factories. In theory, they were supposed to be easier, but I never got a click. My chat, such as it was, didn't work, my jokes failed, my appearance didn't help, being small and looking much younger than I was. I had better luck with some of the younger middle classes, or what I thought at the time were the middle classes. Up at Stanwix.

The poshest, biggest, most impressive houses of all were quite near us, between St Ann's Hill and Stanwix, on Etterby Scaur, overlooking the River Eden, huge detached houses with bells on ropes, the sort of houses I imagined Just William lived in. I used to go carol singing there when quite young, thinking that people living there must be ever so rich, so they are bound to give us some money, but they never did. At one end was Grosvenor College, a fee paying school for thickish boys, who wore black and white uniform. At the other end, nearest us, was Nazareth House. This was a huge building run by frightening looking nuns who wore black with big white wimples on top who often came round our estate, collecting for Catholic charities. They looked after what we assumed were naughty boys, but I think they were mainly orphans. I once played football there, inside, a seven a side game against the boys.

Many years later, I read that there were several Nazareth Houses all over the country, and some of them had been accused of abusing the children in their care who had then been sent to Australia. I'm not sure if Carlisle's was one of them. Today, the building houses Austin Friars, one of the best regarded, most successful schools in Cumbria.

I never knew any girls who lived on Etterby Scaur. The houses all seemed to be lived in by elderly people, or institutions, so you had to go further on, up Etterby Street, to Stanwix itself, to meet the nicer class of likely girls.

Through Ian and Mike who lived at Stanwix, Reg and I used to go most Saturday evenings and hang around the Brampton Road area. There was a girl called Hazel Glue we all ogled, very pretty, great figure, who lived in Croft Road. We waited around outside her house, hoping she would come out and talk to us, which often she did, just to humour us, then her real boy friend would roar up in a sports car and whisk her off.

We discovered a sort of youth club which was being held on Saturday evenings in a large wooden hut in the garden of a big house on Brampton Road. I think it was meant to be educational, or perhaps religious in intent, some rich woman providing well brought up local girls with soft drinks and biscuits and a nice, safe place to meet together and play harmless games. Parents allowed their younger teenage girls to go there, as the woman was well known and it was in her garden, not a public place, safe from any rough youths from council estates. Reg and I used to gatecrash it, then put the lights out. The girls were mainly at private schools, such as Red Gables, who wore green uniforms, or St Gabriel's, who wore blue, and Wykeham House who wore bright purple. All of them modest fee-paying schools, but with very imposing uniforms, for the sort of girls who hadn't managed to pass the Eleven Plus and get into the High School. At the time, they seemed rather classy, Carlisle's answer to Roedean or Cheltenham Ladies College. Once the lights went out, some of these girls were not quite as classy as they might have appeared, more than willing to engage in kiss chases and a bit of fumbling.

A lot of the Stanwix girls were of course at the High School, such as the Atkinson sisters, Joan and Tricia. Their father was a lawyer and they had a lovely house where they often had a few friends in, when their parents were away. We were not always invited, but we would barge in, hoping to get our hands on their dad's drinks, and anything else available.

They once called for me, in Caird Avenue, to invite me to a proper party. I could see them getting out of a car outside our house, walking down our little front path, about to knock at the front door. I was so shocked by the sight of them that I panicked with embarrassment. How had they found out where I lived? That was my first thought. I hadn't lied about where I lived, but I certainly hadn't gone around telling Stanwix girls I lived on a council estate. I dashed into the parlour and crouched down beside my dad. He was in his bed, eating peanuts, bits of the shells clinging to the hairs on his chest and the front of his vest. He didn't know what the hell was going on.

I shouted to my mother that I wasn't in, telling her to keep quiet and not answer the door, but before I could stop them, my sisters had got to the front door and were opening it, all smiles and hellos, inviting les Atkinson gels to step inside. Luckily, my mother shouted that I wasn't at home, so the the Atkinsons declined the offer, saying they were just delivering an invitation for me.

There was another Brampton Road person whom we encouraged to have parties when his parents were away. This was Grant Aitken, a big, cheerful bloke, a great sportsman who later became a professional golfer. Then there was Laurence Fisher who was at the

The Japanese Gardens on Stanwix Bank.

Grammar School, a year below me. He lived on a big house at the end of Stanwix Bank and was very generous with his parents' hospitality.

Nothing of course happened at these parties, nor when boys and girls sat cuddling together on a bench in the Japanese Gardens or in Bitts Park, or even if they got into a clinch against a hedge or up an alleyway. I mean nothing of a truly sexual nature. I never personally knew a boy or a girl in Carlisle in the 1950's who was not a virgin up to the age of eighteen, and more likely up to the age of 21. We heard stories of course, people boasted, and at least once a year there was a rumour about some High School girl who had disappeared, who had fallen, been forced to leave school prematurely, gone away some-where, reputedly to have, gulp, a baby. But it was very very rare - and also very shameful.

It was mostly petty fumbling and heavy petting, messing around amongst the low numbers on the rating scales. Number One was a kiss. Number Two was feeling her breasts. Number Three was getting your hand up her skirt, hoping to feel her fanny, or 'finnin' her, as it was called in Carlisle, or 'finger pie' in Liverpool. Number Four was when she tossed you off. Number Five, that was going the whole hog, the full treatment. No one I knew got to Number Four, never mind

94

Number Five.

There were variations on these numbers, in different parts of Carlisle at different times, as there were throughout the land amongst all teenagers, so I discovered later. Perhaps all cultures have forms of the same thing, with their own slang or euphemisms to denote the stages in the sexual stakes.

Birth control pills did not of course exist. Condoms did, but we were too scared, too embarrassed to even think of going into a chemist and trying to buy any. All we did was tell jokes about johnnies, rubbers, as if we knew what they really were, pretending we had a packet in our inside pocket, ever handy, in case we struck lucky, which we never did. I would probably have run a mile, if some girl had allowed me to get to Four or Five.

When I got into the Upper Sixth, there was a youth club in one of the old lanes we used to go to called the Garrett Club. It was frequented by Grammar and High School fifth and sixth formers. I think it might have been sponsored or somehow run by the council's education department, who had made the premises available as a meeting place for the city's sixth form students.

I knew quite a few High School girls, such as the Atkinson sisters and others I only knew by sight. I had played at the High School in a scratch hockey team, which was mainly the Grammar School's 1st XV rugby team, pretending we could play hockey, just for a chance to get into the High School itself and meet some of the girls.

Another meeting place was Thurnhams, the book shop and stationer, which was then in English Street, opposite the C3 bus stop. Sixth form boys and girls would hang around outside, or inside, pretending to look at books, but really for each other. The Library at Tullie House was also a good place to spot and perhaps chat to girls. I often went there, telling my mother I was going to the Ref to do some homework, or a bit of serious studying, can't get any peace and quiet in this house. The Ref was also a popular haunt for several of Carlisle's tramps or elderly homeless. Despite their scruffy appearance and derelict condition, they would make a point of getting out their specs, opening wide a newspaper, pretending to read it, then fall asleep and start heavily snoring. They were always furious when a bossy librarian told them off or ordered them out, denying that they were asleep. It gave us an excuse to exchange amused looks and knowing glances with any likely High School lasses. One Saturday evening, at a do in the Garrett club, I spotted a girl called Margaret Forster. I already knew about her because she was said to be the High School's star pupil, a right blue stocking, who thought only of her studies, so I'd gathered. She looked attractive to me, so I thought I'd chance my arm and I asked her if she fancied a dance.

'Certainly not,' she said. 'In fact there's nothing I would like less. I hate dancing...'

And with that, she was off, leaving the Garrett Club.

I don't think I talked to her again - for perhaps two years, though I often saw her from afar, heard about her from other people. She clearly had better, more serious, more worthwhile things to do in her life than mess around or waste time with stupid, silly boys.

Chapter Ten

Varsity Chaps

I sat my A levels in 1952, aged 18. They didn't give grades in those days, unless you got a distinction, though you could find out later through the school what your marks had been. I passed all three of my subjects - English, History and Geography - nothing startling, but comfortably enough, with a mark in each of about 55-60, which today would count as three B's.

I then found myself going to Durham University. I know I said that about going from the Creighton to the Grammar, as if I was in a dream, had no hand it, but the same sort of thing occured. I have no memory of looking at lists, thinking now which university should I apply to, what are the rules and conditions, where might I get in, what should I study. I knew so little myself about the system, nor of course did my parents. I left it to the school who said I should apply to Durham. They were sending them there by the charabanc at the time, mostly to the same college, University College. Presumably good contacts must have been made for at least a dozen boys from the Grammar School were already there, and had not yet been chucked out. The college seemed happy enough with them. So Durham was the first and only place I applied to.

You had to fill in what your father's occupation was, so I asked him what I should put, which was how I came to know he was a Higher Clerical Officer (Retired through ill health). You had to have references as well, so my mother said put down the minister of our church, Warwick Road Presbyterian. I said not him, he's boring, and he doesn't know me anyway, but I did.

Couldn't think of anyone else. Working class kids did have a problem describing what their dad did and finding a suitable professional sounding reference.

During my final term, I went over to Durham for an interview in the Castle and saw a moral tutor called Dr Thomson who was lounging in his study on a sofa, with music playing in the background, palm-like plants flapping away, lots of Turkish looking rugs and carpets around. For some reason we got talking about opera, about which I knew bugger all. Perhaps I'd boasted about having been to the Edinburgh Festival. It didn't seem to be a proper interview, just an idle chat, so I didn't know what to make of it, but when my A levels came through, all the bumf appeared from Durham, and off I went, along with Brian Cooke, who had come from the Creighton with me, Bobby Leslie, Nipper Ellis Johnny Howe, and some others, including Ian Johnson, one of my Stanwix friends, though he was going to a different Durham College, St Chads.

Before I departed, the minister of the Warwick Road church asked to see me at his Manse, which was a poky semi somewhere in Stanwix. He was the minister I'd always thought boring and his church dreary. I thought it might be a moral talk, telling me to keep off the women and booze. He then presented me with a £10 note, to spend on anything I needed, as a reward from the Church for getting into university, from some fund which he controlled. Wasn't that kind, after all that moaning I'd done about his church.

Almost everybody in our Upper Sixth form seemed to be going off to some sort of university. It appeared to be what happened, how it was. I don't think I was really aware that in the 1950's I was in an elite minority with only about 4% of eighteen year olds going on to Higher Education. Now it's getting near 44 %. And the aim is eventually to have half the population going to university, or similar. All must have prizes, and if not prizes, letters after their names.

Two of my best friends, Reg and Mike Thornhill, neither of whom had done as well as they had been expected to do at A levels, had decided to stay on for a third year and try Oxbridge. (And both eventually got into Oxford - Mike to Balliol and Reg to St Catherine's.) Dicky Wilson was already in at Oxford, having won a scholarship to Queen's at the age of seventeen. Brian Donaldson, whose relations we stayed at in Edinburgh, went to Cambridge. So that was four from my exact year, in the Arts Sixth, who went to Oxbridge, plus around another ten who went to other universities. Not bad, for a little provincial grammar school in the 1950's.

There was also Fred Tiffin who as far as I remember got stuck in the Remove for a year, then suddenly woke up, started working and got into Cambridge to read History. Some also went on to university from the Science Sixth, but I didn't know them as well, apart from Jack Routledge who also went to Cambridge. His father was a science master at school.

University College, Durham, founded 1832, was and is situated in the Castle, all suitably ancient with courtyards and towers and galleries. It did have the feeling and appearance of an Oxbridge college, not that I'd ever seen one at the time. Durham prided itself on being totally residential, on the collegiate system. There was a quite a lot of ex-public school boys, though nowhere near as many as today, who had tried and failed to get into Oxbridge who arrived with a bit of a chip on their shoulder, feeling they were having to make do with second best. I couldn't understand this mentality, not having tried anywhere else, and felt thrilled to be there.

I loved it right from the beginning, but the best feeling of all was because I was starting from scratch on equal terms with everyone else. I had never felt at the Grammar School that I belonged, knew how things worked. And at the Creighton, I had recently arrived back from Scotland and felt lost for a long time. At Durham, coming from different schools all over England, none of us knew what to expect, and no one knew us. We were all starting together, at square one. If anything, coming from Carlisle, we did have a slight advantage, as there were several Old Carliols already at Castle, such as Pete Ross and the Cartner twins, from whom we could find out things. Durham seemed enormous, with so much to learn, colleges and departments and buildings to explore, but it wasn't really, not compared to its size today. There were only 1500 students at Durham itself in 1952 - compared with about 12,000 today - spread around six men's colleges and three for women. We were technically the Durham Colleges in the University of Durham. King's College in Newcastle, which was much bigger than us, was also part of Durham University, till it broke away and became a separate university.

You had to wear a gown for all lectures, and for dinner in Hall, and to see your tutor. I bought a college blazer and scarf, as everyone did. I eventually bought a suit as well, the first in my life, from Burton's on the Viaduct while home in Carlisle. It was in grey charcoal, the height of cool. I wore it for years till the seat was so shiny it shone. I could never afford what all students wore in the 1950's, the absolute must, proof that you were a varsity chap - a duffel coat. How I longed for one. Instead, when taking a girl out and wanting to impress, I borrowed one from Edmund Vardy - Binks - who lived below me in the Keep. Sometimes, I have to admit, without telling him first, which pissed him off as he had to stay in.

Coming back to Carlisle for the Christmas vac, in my college scarf and blazer, I got a job at the Post Office, as everyone did. The sorting office in Junction Street was a riot of university scarves with everyone, boys and girls, flaunting their college colours, boasting about all the drinking they'd been doing, the essay crises they'd had. I think it took me about two years to realise how naff it was to wear a college scarf.

It was a dawdle working at the Post Office, easy money, rounds could be finished early, so you could go home, or walk about the town, till you clocked off. The regular postmen didn't want you to finish too quickly, or it would show them up. Going on sorting duties was not such a skive, as the work kept on pouring in, but it was inside so you didn't get wet or cold. On the rounds, there was a festive air, jumping on and off old lorries which had been hired by the Post Office for the Christmas rush.

I worked on the Post Office every Christmas during my Durham years, as most students did. The only awful part was one Christmas, unbeknown to me, I found myself working beside my mother. She had also applied to be a Christmas casual and got taken on and was one week in the same sorting department, much to my embarrassment. She would ask me things, what names meant, where streets were. Despite all her years in Carlisle, she still didn't know her way around.

We students on vac hung around the Milk Bar in Devonshire Street when not working, trying to be intellectual and arty. Many of us, such as Peter Gannon who was at Oxford and seemed ever so worldly, smoked Gauloises or strange smelling foreign cigarettes. I've never smoked, anything, in my life, thanks mainly to having asthma. There were of course no drugs, certainly not. I had not even heard of such things.

The scene later moved on when the Fresco opened in Cecil Street which had a real cappuccino machine, the first I'd seen in Carlisle. It seemed very expensive, so you had to spin a small cup out for hours, but ever so classy.

We still went drinking at the Near Boot but also came into town and went to the Friars in Devonshire Street, which was where several of the younger masters at the Grammar hung out. Now that we had left school, we got to know them better, and some were surprisingy human.

Getting Christmas work at the Post Office was easy, but getting some sort of job in Carlisle for the long summer vac, that was very hard. It hung over me during the whole of the summer term, writing endless letters, hoping to be fixed up the minute I arrived back in Carlisle in June. Otherwise, what could you do till October. With no money there would be no holiday, no fun, nowhere to go, nothing to do.

During term time, I was quite well off. I got a generous award of £210 a year from Carlisle Education Committee, thank you very much, as all Carlisle students did, who had got into a university. Everything was paid for, maintenance as well as tuition fees. A large cheque arrived at the beginning of each term, a Midland Bank cheque which I presumed when it first came had to be put into the Midland Bank in order to be used, not realising it could be paid in anywhere. My parents had never had a cheque book or used a bank, why should they, when they had no savings.

During term time, it covered all my expenses, including a lot of drinking at the college bar and the Buffalo's Head. I don't remember ever being in debt, until my very last term, or having to borrow from home. I did send my washing home every week to my mother in Carlisle, being too mean to use a proper laundry - launderettes had not of course been invented - and she returned the clean clothes, along with a large piece of home made ginger bread.

I sent my best white shirt and Van Heusen collars to the real laundry, to get them stiff, as my mother always mucked them up. For college hops or dances, or at the Town Hall or one of the hotels, one always wore a pristine white shirt. The collars were detachable, kept on by studs. I found that I could re-use them by turning them inside out. My collar studs were my father's. He had no use for them any more, being an invalid.

During the vacation, there was no cheque or income coming in, (although the grant did include a notional vacational allowance) to finance drinking and going to dances, hence the desperate need for a holiday job. I so envied my Stanwix friends who through family contacts managed to get cushy vac jobs, such as helping out at the Golf Course or Carlisle Airport. Yes, Carlisle did have an airport in the 1950's, struggling along as ever, announcing new wonderful services which never happened. Ian Johnson once got a job there unloading luggage, thanks to a family contact. He was dead cushty, as there was only ever one plane a day, if that. 'Cushty' was another expression which had just come back to me. I was surprised, many years later, hearing it on 'Only Fools and Horses', as I'd imagined it was a purely Carlisle term.

The only job hope for me was to apply for the sort always available - unskilled labouring, despite my lack of a suitable physique. After a lot of knocking on wooden doors in builders yards, queuing up in make shift offices, I got a labouring job at Niven's wood yard at the beginning of Dalston Road, near where the

Cumberland News now has its offices..

My job at Niven's was loading wood, wheeling barrows of off-cuts, humping bags of sawdust. I was knackered by bait time and counted the minutes till it was over each day. It was so noisy, so you had little chat or contact with the other workers. A lot of the work was on my own, given a yard or a dump to clear and left to get on with it.

During another holiday Mr Adamson, my old violin teacher, did fix me up for a few weeks - so I take back that I had no family contacts. I was a van boy, helping the driver of a Rington's tea van as he went round the country districts, delivering tea. That was all that was delivered, packets of tea, so goodness knows how it was commercially viable. There were endless types of door-to-door deliveries in the 1950's, even to relatively poor areas, which all came to an end in the 1960's, by which time Carlisle's first super-markets had appeared.

In another long vac, I got a labouring job with Carlisle Corporation, in their Direct Labour department They were building their own council houses, up at Morton. Every time I drive that way today, I look with pride at the homes I helped to create with my own hands. I used to tell that to my children. Yes, with these little white hands, they have seen service.

I was a hod carrier. Not one of those brawny ones who could fly up ladders with about a dozen bricks on his hod, held high on his shoulder. I needed about a dozen trips, taking one brick at a time.

Working for the Corporation building department was much more social and enjoyable, if back breaking. I was assigned to a team, serving two or three bricklayers, mostly middle aged and very friendly, interested in who I was and the fact that I was at university. I always tried to keep this quiet, when doing vac jobs, not wanting to be seen as someone just passing through who might be thought to consider himself superior. I can remember one called Pineapple Balls, or Chunky Balls, who for years afterwards would shout from roofs as I happened to pass by, ask me how I was getting on. Several showed off about their sex life, telling me what they did to the wife last night. 'I put my hand across on her minge, like, dead hairy and that...' I would quickly try to change the subject. Another gave me some advice for when I was married, saying the best time for sex with your wife was when she is five months pregnant, as she would then relax.

We had our bait and dinner breaks in a make-shift canteen, a wooden and tarpaulin hut, where a massive copper boiler would be bubbling away all morning, providing hot water for tea. A very old gadgy was in charge of this, a pensioned off labourer who had come back to help out. They were always playing tricks on him, winding him up.

I got to know several of the other labourers, some not much older than me, full time labourers, not students, who were in it for life. One of them, a fading Teddy Boy, still with his quiff in place, took me back to where he lived in a little terrace house off Corporation Road, all damp and threadbare, one of those slum terraces knocked down when they created Castle Way. In it, crouching almost in a corner, was his wife and a kid, which I never realised he had. I wondered how he was going to get through life, provide for them, on his miserable wage. Most of all I thought about the dreariness of doing the same manual job, year after year. Yet he seemed an intelligent enough bloke, not stupid or half witted. Many of the bricklayers struck me as decidedly clever. It all seemed so unfair, unequal, when they were capable of so much. It made me realise how lucky I had been, managing to get on a conveyor belt which was transporting me, so I presumed, so I hoped, to a better more satisfying job in life. I still, however, had no idea what I would do. If asked, I would have said I'm hoping to become a teacher, saying it because I knew it would please my Mum.

Working on the buildings was hellish in the rain and cold, for you had to carry on, unless it was a total downpour. But when the sun came out, I got stripped to the waist and after three months hard graft, I had the best tan I've ever had.

The best paid vac job I got, though not the one which turned out the most important for me, was the following year when at last I got taken on by the Ribble buses. There was a long waiting list to be a bus conductor, and you had to be a certain age, but it was the one most desired by all Carlisle students in the 1950's.

The Ribble company had a proper training scheme, including a residential week-end at Preston, at their HQ. I went with Bobby Leslie, who had been at the Grammar School and was now at Durham with me. We were put in digs for the week-end, somewhere near Deepdale, Preston North End's football ground, for I remember walking round it, thinking how much bigger and grander it was than Brunton Park. We had tests at the end, which were really quite nerve wracking, then we lined up, had a passing out parade.

Working as a bus conductor on the Ribble in Carlisle meant you had to wear uniform, which quickly got very shiny, carry a huge leather money bag and an equally heavy ticket machine which had to be altered all the time, according to the fare stage. I remember the first week or so thinking I'd never cope, there was so much to think about, plus the bell to ring, passengers to chase to stop them getting off without paying, and of course keep an eye out for an Inspector who might appear at any moment from behind a hedge, jump out and stop the bus. Passengers who have not paid think they will be the only one to get it in the neck, but the bus conductor got most of the blame.

Working on a city centre route, especially during the Glasgow Fair week, was chaotic, with buses packed, roads jammed, but the time did pass quickly, as there was so much to do. If you got a country run, out to Cummersdale, that was much quieter and easier. I can still remember the stage numbers and names on that run, such as Brow Nelson, a name you didn't see on any buildings or signposts.

On one of my shifts, on the Longsowerby run, I happened to notice sitting upstairs, all on her own, was Margaret Forster, the girl from the High School I had previously tried to chat up at the Garret Club. Showing off, being Big Mick, trying to impress, I said don't worry, pet, you don't have to pay, I'll let you off, and went downstairs again, keeping a good eye out in case an Inspector called.

She followed me down, almost at once, and insisted on paying, despite my protests. She certainly wasn't going to be let off, cheating the system. She handed over her fare and got off at her stop, without ever a glance back at me on the bus, standing on the platform, trying to look cool, a man of the world.

Chapter Eleven

Teenagers Arrive

One of the significant developments in Carlisle in the 1950's, in fact in the whole of England, Europe, the world of Western Civilisation as we know it, was the arrival of teenagers.

I told my own children about this, when they became teenagers, and of course they didn't believe it. How could teenagers 'arrive' when surely they were always there, ie people aged between four-teen and nine-teen? Technically true, but teenagery as a culture, with its own separate styles, fashions, music, market-place, was unknown to previous generations, until the mid 1950's.

I expected, as I was growing up, that I would eventually emerge pretty much like my father, not him in particular, because of his condition, but like almost all fathers who had gone before. I would gradually change from being a child into adulthood, the traditional signals including starting to wear his overcoat, putting on his collar studs, as I was already doing, plastering his Brylcream on my hair, getting it cut at the same place, the Co-op barber, as he had done, and

Above: Me as an undergrad at Durham in college blazer and tie - before I realized how naff it was to wear your college colours

in the same style, looking and behaving and acting very much like him, till one day I would realise I'd done it, the metaphorphosis was complete, I'd become an adult. I would hardly be aware of any separate intermediary stage, because there wasn't one.

The Teddy Boys were an early sign of the changes taking place, when youths affected a special style of dress not shared by adults, but the real catalyst was pop music.

We had enjoyed singing along to Pat Boone and Guy Mitchell and other American singers with their soppy or silly early 1950's songs, even while mocking them. There were British versions of these American singers, like Dickie Valentine and David Whitfield, who had been popular as well, though they tended to sing in a mid Atlantic accents, wear shiny suits on stage, tell us we were a lovely audience.

The three defining dates for the arrival of what became known as rock n' roll was firstly April 1954 when Bill Haley and his Comets produced 'Rock Around the Clock'. It took about a year for it to have any effect but when it was used as the theme tune for a film called Blackboard Jungle, young audiences across the USA and then the UK started dancing in the aisles and tearing up the seats. When it came to Carlisle - I think the Botchy cinema, not the Lonsdale - there were equally exhuberant audiences of young persons, jiving away. Jiving took over from the quick step as the fast dance, the one to show off with, get to grips with a girl and twirl her round. I was quite good at it, so I liked to think at the time, though when I have demonstrated the steps later, at family parties, everyone cowers in embarrassment. Places like the Crown and Mitre, which considered themselves a superior dance venue, would not at first allow jiving, no more than they had allowed in Teddy Boys. But at the County and the Cameo, the new dances and culture caught on quickly. For a while, there was a strange intermediary stage in some dance halls where at one end there would be couples jiving, with people crowding in a circle to watch them doing it, while at the far end of the dance hall, old fashioned quick steps and waltzes would still be taking place, two cultures, two generations, enjoying themselves in the same room at the same time, but in a different way.

JOHN DAVIES
HUNTER DAVIES
MICHAEL BATEMAN

present

The BLUE DEVILS
North-Eastern Skiffle Champions

WEARMOUTH BRIDGE
7pm Thursday 20 March

Refreshments provided

Bill Haley was fleshy, flabby with a stupid quiff, not exactly a young sex symbol, but then came the second big event, the arrival of Elvis Presley. By May 1956, his Heartbreak Hotel was top of the charts in fourteen countries.

The third and perhaps most influential development was skiffle, which came in just before so called rock 'n' roll. In Britain, the important date was January 1956 when Lonnie Donnegan's single Rock Island Line became a surprise number one hit. He had recorded it back in 1954 on an LP record (long player - don't say you've forgotten) with Chris Barber, but it took a year for it to appear as a single, and then it shot through the charts.

In Carlisle, as in all parts of the country, skiffle groups emerged almost overnight, like mushrooms, sprouting up in schools and youth clubs. The big attraction of skiffle was that you could join in, take part, without being able to read music, play an instument, or even have a proper instrument. I found myself on a washboard one evening in Rickerby Park near to the Suspension Bridge where an impromptu skiffle concert was taking place. At Durham, along with another friend, Mike Bateman, I organised skiffle parties, hiring local skiffle groups to perform in rooms we had booked in pubs.

Like all other teenagers of the time, I was desperate to have tight trousers, which of course my father had never worn, so there was no point in borrowing his. Many parents would not allow it, so that boys would often have their trousers narrowed secretly, then hide them at a friend's house, changing into them when going to a dance or a party. Girls did much the same, hiding their more extravagaent teenage styles from their parents. There was a woman in Caird Avenue, just along from us, who would tighten your trousers for a few shillings.

There slowly grew up a separate market for teenage clothes and styles, aimed purely at teenagers, which had not existed before. Radio and then TV produced programmes just for teenagers, such as Six Five Special. In Carlisle, the Milk Bar and the Fresco were the places teenagers congregated, along with students. Dance halls began to specialise in teenage evenings, such as Bonds.

I had several girlfriends during my first two years at Durham, and also at home in Carlisle, during the vacations. Being a student did help to impress Carlisle girls still at school in their sixth forms, waiting to get into university. In Carlisle I went out with a girl called Joan Scott who later went to Oxford.

I also went out with a girl whose name I can't now remember but her father had become the new manager of Binns. A shop we never used, being too expensive, though not quite as posh as Bulloughs, which was for the real quality, the county types. My mother didn't go to Jespers either, for similar reasons.

Whenever I had got any new school clothes, they had either come from the Co-op or from a really cheap ex-army surplus store in Rickergate, now long gone.

The daughter of the Binns manager was very attractive, classy and elegant, as one would expect, having such a pater. I felt I had gone up a notch, socially, just by being seen with her. I don't know why she went out with me, apart from the fact that she was a stranger to the town and was finding her way around.

She wasn't a student but a secretary in some office. She lived in a big house at Burgh by Sands and one week-end she invited me to visit her - and stay the night. Oh rapture. Did I boast, did I tell everyone I'd landed on my feet.

I rode out to her house on my Raleigh Lenton sports, taking my jamas, a new pair, especially washed, and clean socks, as my socks did often rather smell in those days. I don't think I had thought about who else might be there, if anyone, and perhaps even imagined we would be alone, so I was quite surprised to see her parents were sitting there, in their living room, obviously not going anywhere. We had a meal all together, which was salad, my least favourite, sat watching TV with them, had a cup of cocoa with them, then I went up to my bedroom and she went to hers. And that was it. Next day, I cycled back to Carlisle - and never saw her again.

I made the most of these various encounters, many years later, flammed them up when writing 'Here We Go Round The Mulberry Bush' which in the novel, not the film, was clearly set in Carlisle. All the girls were fictional, or at least an amalgam of several put together. Yet I still keep meeting people in Carlisle today who say I went out with them in the 1950's, because they recognized themselves in the book, so they say.

The other day I was interviewed on Radio Cumbria by a reporter I thought must be about my age, or the age I like to think I am. After the interview, he said oh, by the way, my Mum used to go out with you. I asked her name, and it was a common Carlisle surname. I said oh yes, give her my regards, but I had no memory of her at all.

Common Carlisle surnames are still with us, like Graham, Wilson, Bell, Johnstone, Thompson, Armstrong. Carlisle people tend not to move around, as much as they do in other parts of the country. When I was at the Creighton, half the class at one time seemed to be called Graham. Looking at today's Carlisle and North Cumbria telephone directory, which I did not long ago, being rather bored, you'll see in the residential section that the Grahams are spread over ten columns, which I estimate must mean that there are well over 1,000 families called Graham in and around Carlisle. No, I didn't count them exactly. I wasn't that bored.

I did go out with a girl called Graham, Cora Graham, for a while. She lived out in the country, near Burgh, and was very blonde, but then that's another mark of true Cumbrians, especially when they are young. You see them up street with their Mams on Saturday mornings, the boys and girls, looking angelic, like little Angels, or at least Anglo-Saxons, betraying the Norse blood which still runs through many Cumbrian families. Later, when they get older, most of these child blonds turn to mousy brown. Cora Graham died tragically when still quite young in a road accident, one of the first people in Carlisle of my age I ever knew who had died. In the Cumberland News today, there are teenage deaths every week, from car or motorbike accidents. In the 1950's, it was very rare, as of course few teenagers had access to motors.

During the long summer vac of 1956, just when life was changing for teenagers generally in Britain, two important events happened to me in Carlisle which affected the rest of my life.

At Durham, my room mate, John Davies, was giving up a little job he had as advertising manager of Palatinate, the student newspaper. I offered to take it on, purely in order to have something to put on my CV, to indicate I had done something at Durham, other than drink, play sport and go out with girls. By going to the Palatinate office, which was then run by a group from Hatfield College, as these things often are, passing jobs around amongst themselves, they all struck me as very ordinary, not to say pretty stupid, certainly no cleverer or more gifted than me. I had never thought of writing anything, either journalism or creative stuff, partly due to the fact that at the Grammar School Sixth, my friend Reg Hill had written such brilliant pieces for the mag that I thought I could never hope to do as well.

Palatinate had a hole in the pages one day, when I went in with some ads I had secured, so I said I would fill it. I wrote a first person column about the day in the life of a boat club hearty, basing it on various half witted boat club, public school types at Castle, complete with bad spelling and lots of vomiting. It went down well, so I did another for the next edition, about a theology student, then I did one as if written by a science student. I called this little series 'A Life in the Day of'. (Twenty years later, I pinched the title, and the basic format, though this time making it serious, when I became editor of The Sunday Times colour mag.)

Having stumbled into journalism, honestly not knowing what I was going to do in life, just by doing this little series, I began to

111

become obsessed by it, writing bits all the time, putting down on paper every little thing that happened to me, however trivial, trying to turn it into an article for publication, or just for my own sake, to see if I could do it.

I decided I wanted to be a journalist though I had no idea how you went about it, or what it would be like to work on a proper newspaper.

Before the next vacation, I wrote to the Editor of the Cumberland News, John Burgess, later Sir John, head of the family which still controls the group. He agreed to see me, which was kind, and fixed a time for me to come to his office when I returned to Carlisle. I thought our little chat went quite well, but at the end, he said I gabbled too much. He hadn't been able to understand half of what I said, due to the way I spoke. Because of that, so he said, I would never make it as a journalist. Very sorry, he had nothing for me.

So I went across the road to the Carlisle Journal. Lucky for me that there existed a rival paper. Today, in Carlisle, it would have been impossible.

I saw the editor and, amazingly, he took me on for the summer hols. I wouldn't get a wage, as such, but he would pay me lineage for every story I got in the paper. I worked out that I would never earn as much as I had got on the Ribble buses, and therefore I was going to be very hard up all summer, unable to go off anywhere on hols, but I thought it would be worth it, just to work on a real paper, and have some real cuttings to prove it.

The second event of importance, at least to me, during that vacation, occurred in June or it may have been July. Which might suggest it couldn't have been all that vital if I can't recall the exact date.

I was walking through Town, going past the City Picture House, on the way to catch the C3 bus to St Ann's Hill. There was a big queue for the cinema, as there almost always was in those days, right along the pavement. At the top of the queue, was a couple of my friends from school, Mike Thornhill and I think Ian Johnston. They were with some girls from the High School, including Margaret Crosthwaite and Margaret Forster. I knew them all, roughly, had done for some years, with being at the Grammar School.

They were in a little group, all together, but not exactly couples, in the sense of couples who had paired off, not that I was aware. Or if I did and they were, I decided to ignore it anyway.

On the spur of the moment, even though I was on the way home, I decided to barge in, joining them at the top of the queue. People behind started muttering and complaining, but I thanked my friends, loudly, for having kept my place. I went in with them, sat down with them, or at least as near them as I could. The cinema was already pretty full, with not many empty seats, but I ended up in the row behind as the four of them had managed to sit together. This didn't put me off and during the film I kept up an inane conversation over their shoulders, trying to be smart and amusing.

When we all came out, I stood around talking to them on the pavement. They had made it pretty clear that I was a bit of an interloper, not having been invited on this particular outing, but I continued to ignore all this, and kept on nattering away.

Eventually, it was obvious they were now about to disperse, going to their various homes or catching their respective buses. And they expected me to do the same, perhaps the sooner the better.

Instead, I found myself asking Margaret Forster if I could walk her home. Amazingly, considering that twice at least in the last couple of years she had repulsed my advances, she said yes. And that was it. I walked her home. It turned out to be a very long walk, one I am still walking . . .

Chapter Twelve

Enter Margaret

I didn't know where Margaret lived, nor did she know where I lived, but she had remembered our encounters, and also watching me play hockey for the Grammar against the High School. She had heard I was home from Durham, having a rest from a dissolute life, which of course I denied.

On the way home with her, I mentioned going to the Edinburgh Festival and the Proms, trying to give myself an artistic, intellectual image, and in passing said how much I loved Sibelius. 'What's he written?' asked Margaret, assuming he was a novelist. That was a relief. She wasn't quite the all round brain box I had been led to believe.

She had finished her A levels and was marking time, waiting for the results. That was probably why she had weakened and accepted my advances, feeling demob happy, wanting a break after all that heavy duty studying. I was lucky, catching her at the right time. If I hadn't gone past the City Picture House that particular evening, if I hadn't pushed my way into the queue, who knows if we would have ever met.

Is life all about luck and chance and happenstance? I don't actually think so. Accidents, disease, that's almost wholly bad luck, over which you have little control. But good luck, I think you can help to make that happen. The more you try, the more chances you have of getting lucky. But back to 1950's Carlisle.

Margaret lived in Longsowerby, at 180 Richardson Street, at the top end, opposite the cemetery, a very neat, immaculate house, especially the garden. The hedges and lawns had been scuplted to within half an inch of their lives by her father, Arthur. He was working at Metal Box, setting off each morning on his bike in his boiler suit, never late, never a day off, oh since Pauline was born. This was a family joke, in the Forster family. Margaret's mother Lily always used to say she bad not been to the pictures since Pauline - Margaret's younger sister - had been born, which was about sixteen years previously. So anything that had not happened for a long time, was not since Pauline was born.

I said good night, on her door step, not being so bold as to attempt a kiss, but arranged to meet again, and then I walked all the way back to St Ann's Hill, in a daze, walking in space, seeing poetry in the litter fluttering around the old Town Hall, going over all the things I'd said, and should have said, and what she said, or appeared to say.

Apparently, I appeared to give the impression that I was from a relatively pukka family, what with letting it slip out that I played the violin, my sisters playing the piano, and we once lived in a big house in Dumfries where I rode a bike down the corridors. I don't remember ever saying the latter, but it was enough to make it a slight surprise for her when she discovered I lived in Caird Avenue, in a council house, just like her's, though not quite as neat and kempt.

Margaret had only been in Richardson Street for about three years. Before that, until she was 14, her family had lived at 44, Orton Road, Raffles, the house in which she had been born. She was very proud of having been born at home, which rarely happened in those days, and always looked upon their Raffles house as her real home, not Richardson Street.

Raffles in the 1950's was not quite the ideal garden estate which

115

it had been when created in the 1930's, and Longsowerby was now thought of as a much nicer council estate, which was why they had moved. They now had an inside lavatory, which they hadn't had at Orton Road. But Raffles was nothing like as rough and depressed as it later became. Last time I passed her Raffles birthplace, a wrecked car had gone through the front hedge, leaving a massive hole; the garden which her father had kept immaculate was completely over run; the downstairs windows were boarded up and the area appeared to be full of drug dens.

It was through Margaret in the long hot summers of 1956 and 1957 - which will always be hot to me, whatever the temperatures really were - that I got to know Cumbria. Forster is one of those true Cumbrian and Border surnames and her family, on all sides, had been here for centuries, unlike my family. I can't believe now that I had never been to Silloth, till I met Margaret. I'd heard about it, of course, from so many Carlisle people, who made it sound like a cross between Blackpool, El Dorado and Disneyland, not of course that Disneyland had been invented. Margaret reminisced about her childhood outings to Silloth, how passengers had been jam packed into each carriage as it left its own platform at Citadel Station, then the excitement of counting all the little stations, till at last they arrived at Silloth.

I was a bit disappointed first time. Silloth seemed so old fashioned, so quiet, not much to do. British Rail was beginning to run down the Silloth line which eventually closed in 1964, but I did grow to love going there. The point of Silloth was not the excitement but getting a 'bit of a blow.' That's what Carlisle people have always said, not expecting anything like heat and sun or similar sybaritic pleasures, but a bracing walk along the front in a howling gale. Margaret introduced me to Skinburness, to a walk around Grune Point which we still do every year, and on it she always tells me the same story, about how she went camping there aged fifteen with some of her girl friends from school, all on their own, miles from anywhere, on a bit of open grass, not a camp site. No parents would allow that today.

When we couldn't afford the train to Silloth, we would go on our bikes out to Glasson Point, then on to Port Carlisle and Bowness, strange little isolated, left-over Solway villages I didn't know existed. If it was pouring, we would take a Ribble bus, back and forwards across town, from terminus to terminus, sitting up at the front upstairs, hoping there would be no one else there by the time we reached the terminus, talking all the time. That's all we did that first long hot summer, talk non-stop. One of the problems about courting in the 1950's was having somewhere to go, preferably dry, preferably inside or under cover, and free or very cheap. No one we knew had a car to drive us anywhere and in families like ours, no one had their own bedroom. Not of course that any parents would have allowed one's boyfriend or girlfriend into a bedroom.

I eventually got invited into her house, on the evenings I walked home with her, and her Mum would make me a cup of Camp coffee, made with milk, and a Carr's sport biscuit, yum yum, before I set off on the long walk back to St Ann's Hill. I didn't see much of her Dad, in fact I tried to keep out of his way, apart from trying to ingratiate myself by talking about Carlisle United, which failed totally.

Apparently, he thought I looked foreign, Spanish or Italian, with my very dark hair which did get very greasy, as I hardly ever washed it. I was unaware at the time of stuff called shampoo, thinking it was just for women. He also didn't approve of the fact that I had got out of National Service, so far, by being a student. Several of my friends from the Grammar, such as Reg, had gone off and were serving the Queen, getting their Nat Service done first, before university. It was already known that my age group would be amongst the last batches to be called up, and I certainly didn't want to be amongst them. On August 4 that first summer - I know the date because we celebrate it every year since - her parents were away, visiting relatives in Scotland, we went off for the whole day to Keswick. It was the most incredible weather, blue skies, cloudless, the sort which makes you realise Lakeland is the best place on the planet. We lay at Friar's Crag, letting the sun go down, and down, till we realised we had missed the last bus. So we set off, about eleven o'clock, to walk back to Carlisle.

After about five miles, I began to feel very tired. After ten miles, I was knackered. After another ten miles, I was on my knees with

Margaret helping me along. The final ten miles I walked in a trance, semi-conscious, except for breaking into a cold sweat and an attempt at a quick dash when we were staggering through Thursby. A lumbering figure had appeared in the dark behind us, shouting something awful which scared me to death, thinking we were about to be murdered. It was only a tramp, whom we had disturbed while sleeping in a hedge. We got back to her house about five in the morning. I think I fell asleep, shattered, in her front room, passing out for a few hours, before dragging myself on to the first bus to St Ann's. Margaret always was stronger, fitter than me. When we went youth hostelling, she usually carried the rucksack, except when we passed through villages or habitation, then I would take it for half a mile or so, pretending to be a real man.

We had two nights once at Grasmere Youth Hostel, which had been excellent, doing lots of long walks. Margaret counted up our monies and reckoned we had just enough for one more night at a Youth Hostel, or we could have a proper meal, and go home this evening. It was up to me - I could decide for both of us. I opted for the meal. I was never forgiven. What it meant, so she said, was that I preferred some horrible pie and chips to another night in her company. It is true that when we were sitting somewhere really fantastic, like the top of Place Fell looking down on Ullswater, she would ask me what I was thinking and before I could stop myself, I did often find myself saying 'A pint and a pie, that's what I really fancy'.

People did wonder what she saw in me, why such a a blue stocking, clever, original, talented, forthright, strong-willed girl should get mixed up with me, her first ever boyfriend. I did wonder that myself, especially when her A level results came through - Distinctions in English and History, plus a pass in Latin. The High School headmistress, Miss Cotterell, sent her actual marks in English and History, which were 95% in each, unheard of for those sort of arts subjects.

For the glory and greatness of the school, and to get her name up in lights for ever, or at least in letters on the wooden honours board in the school hall, she really did have to try for Oxbridge, so all her teachers said. I thought if she does that, and gets in, mixing with the cream of the nation's youth, brilliant golden boys from the top public schools, many of them with flaxen hair, probably even their own shampoo, I wouldn't stand a chance and never see her again.

To celebrate her excellent A level results, her dad Arthur came home from work one day, got off his bike, put his hand in his boiler suit and presented her with a ten shilling note. 'Here y'are lass.' We were all amazed, especially as he was from that generation who believed girls did not need to be educated and would be just as well off as a cracker packer at Carr's.

I immediately worked out a good way of spending it. I said let's go out on the bus to Wetheral and have a slap-up meal at the Fantails. This had not long opened and was the most fashionable, smartest local restaurant, not that there was much competition in the 1950's. I put on my best charcoal grey suit and borrowed Arthur's best umbrella.

I asked for the menu when we got there and was horrified to see the expense of even the humblest dish. I had imagined that her Dad's ten bob note would have been more than enough to cover a proper tuck-in. It was all the money I had, so I steered her towards the cheapest item, which was a cheese omelette. She has always liked omelettes so that was OK, but I hate them, ugh, so boring.

When the bill came it had somehow jumped to twelve shillings. I hid the bill from Margaret and ushered her to the front door of the Fantails which is on the top of a flight of stone steps, while I went off to see the owner manager. He was a very posh, fleshy man, with thick grey hair, all smily and charming, at least up to that moment. Confronted by a customer unable to pay the bill, his smile immediately faded. I had visions of having to wash up. I apologised profusely, explained the reasons for the celebration, but he wasn't impressed. He wanted me to leave some security, and come back and pay the difference tomorrow, but I didn't have anything. I emptied all my pockets, giving him everything, the ten bob note, plus some coppers for the bus home.

I was eventually allowed out. I rejoined Margaret at the top of the stairs, holding Arthur's umbrella, twirling it to show how debonair, what a man of the world, I know how to treat a girl, when the umbrella came to pieces, bits flying down the steps. That would be more expense and Arthur would be furious.

Opposite, hanging around the Wetheral bus stop, were some uncouth local youths, who had been watching me with the brolly and smart suit, thinking what a prick. How they roared.

We had to walk back the five miles home to Carlisle during which time I admitted what had happened. Next day, having borrowed two bob, I had to trail out to Wetheral again. I remember thinking one day, when I'm rich, I'll buy the Fantails and sack that bastard. We did have lots of rows, not about that subject, just stupid, silly arguments about nothing really, though it seemed very heated and depressing at the time. 'You said this, oh no I didn't, it was you who said it, don't you listen to yourself.'

A lot of our arguments were about my lack of punctuality. Margaret's idea of catching a train on time means being on the platform, all ready, half an hour before the train is due. My idea of good timing is to arrive and jump on the train, just as it's leaving. We used to meet at Burton's corner, still there, which was handy for both our buses, coming into town. I was very often late, or I got the rendezvous wrong, thinking we were meeting outside the City, so she would stand at Burton's for hours, and be absolutely furious when I eventually turned up, maintaining I'd been standing at the City, which was usually a lie.

Sometimes we met at Atkinson House in Abbey Street, named after Herbert Atkinson, a well known Alderman of the 1940's and 5O's. It had been refurbished and re-opened as some sort of student centre where you could go, do some quiet study, join things, hear about various student events and facilities, or just make yourself some tea and lie on the couch, which was what I usually wanted to do.

Carlisle had suddenly begun to realise its potential as a student centre, and there was even talk of perhaps having its own university some day, to serve the County. In 1950, the Art College had moved from Tullie House to Holmeacres, a big house with grounds off the Brampton Road, and was becoming well known and well respected. John Bratby was one of the tutors for a time. Sheila Fell RA went there, before going to London. Then the new Technical College had been opened in Victoria Place in 1954 which was attracting lots of students.

Alas, when all the new universities came to be established in the 1960's, Carlisle didn't get one. Lancaster, so it was said, got one instead. It wasn't till the 1990's that various campuses and branches of colleges and universities situated elsewhere began appearing in Carlisle. Now it looks as if Carlisle might have its own proper university one day soon, to serve the City and Cumbria, which will be a welcome addition to the City, if only fifty years late.

Margaret, like me, had the same problem finding any sort of summer holiday job to earn herself some money. The worst she'd had was at the Steam Laundry down Warwick Road, just pastBrunton Park, sorting dirty clothes. The whole place was filthy, noisy, unbearably hot and the women who worked there foul mouthed. She'd also worked in Santa's Grotto at the Co-op in Botchergate, which was also dirty and unpleasant, and for a short while she'd assisted a dentist who drank and was very bad tempered.

But in the summer of 1956 she got a part time summer job at Marks and Spencer which was an eye opener - but in a different way. She was astounded by how clean and well organised it was behind the scenes, unlike the other places she'd worked, with an excellent canteen and a hair salon provided for the staff. The only boring part was the actual work, serving on the knicker counter. In those days, Marks, like all big shops, had a sales assistant behind every counter, who took the money, there and then, rather than customers having to trail to a pay desk in another part of the store

Paying in shops in the 1950's was a very complicated business. I used to love as a child going into Liptons and seeing the overheard little cables which conveyed the cash canisters, sending them whizzing and clattering all round the shop. I longed to pull the handles, and start the mechanism. In Binns and the Co-op there were chutes, little tunnels running between the floors, which seemed to blow or suck the little metal capsules which carried the cash. What was the point of it all? Presumably there was a central cashier, hidden away in the bowels or in a little cubicle, who checked all bills, took the money, worked out the change, then sent it whooshing and clattering back, whence it had come. Hard to believe it was quicker than allowing ordinary staff to handle money, but it reduced the chances of fiddling.

During that first long summer going out with Margaret, exploring Cumbria, finding out that girls had the same sorts of problems getting work as boys, I discovered it was she who had petitioned the Headmistress of the High School not to give a half day holiday for that visit of Arsenal to Brunton Park in 1951. Spoilsport.

I also discovered that we had nearly met, many years earlier in Motherwell, of all places. It turned out that we had relations in exactly the same road in Motherwell, Bellshill Road, where my Grandma Brechin lived and also her Aunty Jean. I had actually played with her cousins, the Wallaces, whom she often used to visit. The chances are that we had been there, at the same time, without realising.

Well, what a coincidence. It seemed a good omen. Fate had been conspiring to bring us together for longer than we had realised. Ahhhh...

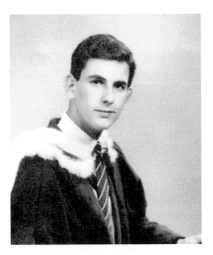

Chapter Thirteen

Oxford in Drag

The offices of the Carlisle Journal were in English Street, near the City Picture House and Jespers, not far from the present Marks and Spencer, backing on to West Walls. They did have a dusty, old fashioned front window display on English Street which had nothing to do with the newspaper itself but displayed envelopes, writing pads and lavatory paper, which was apparently a side line run by one of the directors.

You entered by a side door, in a side passage, and then went upstairs and reached a series of ancient little rooms with wooden floors and bare walls. That's how I remember them. The printing works were on the ground floor.

The paper had had a long and distinguished history, far older than the Cumberland News, having been founded in 1798, which makes it one of England's, not just Cumbria's, oldest newspapers. In the nineteenth century, it had the largest circulation of any journal in Cumberland, Westmorland and Dumfriesshire, covering all the towns between Annan down to Penrith and across the area from Hexham to

Above: I graduated in 1957 - BA (Dunelm).

Whitehaven. It was always known as a staunch Liberal paper. By the time I joined it in the mid 1950's it was a shadow of its former self, with a small staff, small circulation, overshadowed by the bigger, more successful, more professional Cumberland News.

The editor of the Journal was Mr Fred Humphrey, OBE, an award he had received for work in the Ministry of Information during the war. The chief reporter was Dick Allen who later joined the Cumberland News as agricultural correspondent. The photographer was a chirpy, cheerful Londoner called Laurie Kemp who was very helpful to me, and is now a well known Carlisle writer. The paper came out twice a week, on a Tuesday and a Friday. Friday was the main paper and it would often run late as the Head Printer liked to go for a drink at The Sportsman Inn on Thursday evenings, then come back and stand in the print room shouting 'Fuck the Duke of Edinburgh'.

The paper was so hard up and so short staffed that often the same stories were used twice - Tuesday's stories reappearing word for word on Friday. I hoped that it would mean I would be paid twice, if my stuff was repeated, but the editor said no, only the once. Ordinary reporters did not get their names in the paper, not like now, when even the smallest story has a whopping by-line.

I sat in one of the little rooms and had access to a rackety old typewriter, which I could only use with one finger - now I have advanced to two - and mainly re-wrote press hand-outs and announcements, or lifted stuff from other publications. When I was allowed out, which wasn't often, it was mainly to flower shows and prize givings where my main job was to write down the list of names and winners correctly, as many of them as possible, the theory being they would all buy copies in order to see their name in the paper

The biggest event I can remember covering was the Penton Sports on the Scottish border. I went there on the bus with Margaret. I dutifully copied down all the winners. In passing, I had noticed during one of the racing events, that a horse pulling a trap had rather reared its head and refused to start. I remember thinking that could have been nasty, if it had got free.

My report, in the Journal, said it had been a successful show,

STYLE and VALUE in LADIES' WEAR
Studholmes of CARLISLE

Carlisle Journal

With which is incorporated the "Carlisle Express and Examiner" and the "Carlisle Evening Journal"

No. 13900 —2nd W.Q.   Registered at the G.P.O. as a Newspaper.   FRIDAY, JULY 11, 1956   Established 1798   PRICE THREEPENCE

QUEEN'S REGRET AT INABILITY TO PAY VISIT

Messages To The Lord Lieut. and Mayor

CIVIC HEAD THANKS ALL WHO HELPED

LETTERS sent from Buckingham Palace on Wednesday, and received yesterday by the Lord Lieutenant of Cumberland, Sir Robert Chance, and the Mayor of Carlisle, Mr. Irving Burrow, express the "deep disappointment" of Her Majesty the Queen that she was unable to carry out her visit to Carlisle.

The letter to the Mayor conveys the thanks of the Duke of Edinburgh for the hospitality extended to him and states: "His Royal Highness was greatly moved by the warmth of the welcome given to him on all sides."

Letter to the Lord Lieutenant

THE FRIENDLY DUKE

STATE "PUB" MEN IN CITY COURT

Five Dealt With: Other Cases Adjourned

FIVE of the 13 former State Inn managers charged with causing valuable securities to be delivered to themselves by false pretence, were dealt with by the Carlisle City Magistrates' Court yesterday, and fines and costs imposed totalled £37 13s.

John James Armstrong,

The Carlisle Journal the day the Queen's visit was cancelled.

grand weather, and then listed all the winners. In the Cumberland News, their report had a big headline saying 'Horse runs amok at Penton'. I hadn't even realised the Cumberland News had been there. I got a bollocking for that, for missing the big story. I denied it had been a big story, just a trivial little incident, with no danger to anyone, but of course that was not the point. I learned two things. First to make the most of anything, even it means flamming it up, in order to get a good intro, and secondly, find out who else is covering the same story, then agree with them, if possible, about what actually happened.

Back at Durham, I continued to work on Palatinate, the student newspaper, and eventually became editor. Meanwhile Margaret took the Oxbridge entrance exams - and was awarded a scholarship to Somerville College, Oxford. In those days, a lot of the big, famous Northern grammar schools were able to enter for what were known as closed scholarships, limited to certain schools, but Margaret had won an open scholarship, meaning it was open to any school, anywhere. She had also won an award at Girton College, Cambridge. She chose the Oxford one because Girton had seemed gloomy,

Gothic and she didn't like the food.

Margaret left school at Christmnas, then in the Spring went off to Bordeaux as an au pair. But before that, she joined me at my 21st birthday party, on Jan 7, 1957, which I held at the Central Hotel on the Viaduct. God, what a dreary, awful evening that was - and it cost me a fortune. Obviously my parents could not have afforded it, so I had saved up from working on the post over Christmas, doing lots of over-time, and decided to treat my closest friends, such as Reg and his girlfriend Pat (now his wife), Mike Thornhill, Ian Johnston, Dicky Wilson, Margaret Crosthwaite and probably a couple of others whose names I have forgotten. I ordered a proper sit-down do, white table cloths, a waiter in uniform, the full works. The dining room was empty and the waiter aged about a 150 with soup stains down his front and the food was appalling. I arrived in a bad temper because, beforehand, I had taken another group of friends, not invited to the sit-down, to have a drink with me at a pub in Fisher Street. I made it clear I'd buy them a drink each, as my treat, expecting they'd have a half of bitter or a Nut Brown Ale, which they all did apart from this one bloke called John . . . . He ordered a whisky, cheeky sod. He wasn't even a particular friend, being in the year below me at the Grammar School, so I don't know why I had invited him. Being Big Mick, I suppose. I'm not mentioning his second name, but I was furious and have not forgotten or forgiven him.

Oxford had told Margaret that she must improve her French, if she wanted to read History, so this was why she had got herself this job as an au pair. Didn't learn much French, but did a lot of washing, cleaning and child minding.

She started at Oxford in the autumn of 1957, while I was still at Durham. We wrote all the time, but I was now more than ever convinced someone would come along and whisk her away, now she was mixing with all those glittering, gilded youths.

I hitch-hiked down to Oxford from Durham as often as I could. Everyone hitch-hiked in those days. In a previous long vac, I had hitch-hiked round France and Germany with my room mate from Durham, John Davies. We were aiming for Tubingen where a German student we had become friendly with at Durham was now studying. We got to Tubingen, knocked on the door of the address we were given. He wasn't there, so we turned round, and hitch-hiked straight back to England. Moving was the thing, experiencing new places, rather than the arrival.

When I hitch-hiked down to see Margaret in Oxford, I slept on the floor of Mike Thornhill's room in Balliol. In those days, women could not entertain male friends after a certain time. One evening, I overstayed by an hour or two, forgetting the time, while visiting Margaret at her room in Somerville College. How was I going to get out without being spotted? I realised I would be seen leaving through the College main entrance, which at that time of night was the only way in or out. I could try and climb a wall, but that would be dangerous. I could stay the whole night, and leave the next morning during normal visiting hours, but that could also be risky, if anyone saw me. We decided the best way to leave and not be noticed or apprehended was through the front lodge - disguised as a woman.

I rolled up my trousers, put on Margaret's coat, wrapped her college scarf round my neck and walked boldly through the lodge gateway. The porter saw me, but said nothing, as female visitors were still allowed in and out at that time. The gateway was badly lit, so that was a help. I avoided saying 'Goodnight' in a high pitched voice, but was tempted.

I walked up Woodstock Road and then turned into an alleyway and rolled down my trousers, took off Margaret's Somerville scarf. There was a couple in the alleyway, in a heavy clinch, and I could see the man had been watching me. This time, I was unable not to say 'Goodnight' to them, in a silly voice. Then I left the alley and went back to Balliol, to sleep on Mike's floor.

What I didn't know was that the bloke kissing the girl goodnight was the editor of Cherwell, the Oxford student newspaper. He'd noticed my hairy legs and realised what I must have been doing, so ran a story about a man escaping from Somerville, disguised as a woman. He didn't know at that time Margaret's name, but later in the week, some kind person at Somerville must have told him or let it slip. This time he flogged the story to the Daily Sketch, a popular tabloid, later bought over by the Daily Mail.

When this story appeared, Margaret was hauled up before the Principal of Somerville, Dame Janet Vaughan, for bringing the good name of the college into disrepute. She had expected higher standards from a Scholar of the College. Margaret got gated for the rest of the term, but as it was near the end of term, that wasn't too worrying.

In her second year, Margaret went into digs, sharing with another girl, Theodora, in a house in Winchester Road, so that made it much easier to visit her.

On my visits to Oxford, when I met her with her chums, especially male chums, I got all chippy and twisted. She became for a while an actress at Oxford, starring in The Caucasian Chalk Circle with Denis Potter. I became convinced I was being looked down upon by some of these bright, clever Oxford types because I was only at a provincial university. It was all in my head, they didn't actually care, if they were even aware of me, but that was how I felt for a while. Very silly.

I decided to stay on for a fourth year at Durham, for various reasons, none of them very logical. I wanted to avoid National Service, that was one reason. When my call-up papers did come, I got my Carlisle doctor to send proof of the awful asthma I had always suffered from. I did have a medical test - and failed it. So I didn't need a fourth year after all.

What I decided to do in my fourth year was a post graduate Diploma of Education, the thinking being that it would give me some sort of qualification. I still had nothing fixed up in the way of a job or training, so at least I could be a teacher, if nothing else turned up. And it would please my Mum.

I also thought that as Margaret was still at Oxford, having another year as a student would somehow fit in with her life better, our holidays would coincide, it would be easier to be together.

But probably the main reason was that I wanted to continue as editor of Palatinate - which I thought would give me a better chance of finding out if I wanted to be a real journalist. And also perhaps discover how you went about it.

The Appointments Board at Durham seemed pretty dopey, as most university appointments boards were and probably still are, full of jobsworths, who don't know how to get a proper job themselves. The person I saw had had no experience of anyone from Durham going on to be a journalist and didn't seem able to help me. I did find out, though, that an ex-student from my own college, so one of the Castle dons told me, had been an editor of Palatinate about six years previously and had gone on to get a job in journalism, a bloke called Harry Evans, but no one knew where he was now working.

Through a friend on the local newspaper, the Durham Advertiser, an Oxford graduate called Michael Bateman with whom I had organised skiffle parties, I discovered that two national newspaper groups had graduate trainee schemes. One was the Westminster Press, which he had joined, and the other was Kemsley Newspapers, which was the better one, owners of The Sunday Times in London and lots of big provincial dailies and evening papers. I decided to send off applications for both, sending my cuttings from Palatinate and the Carlisle Journal.

I didn't know whether either would come off, so through the Appointments Board I also applied for the usual milk-round type jobs, mostly management training schemes, one of which resulted in an interview with a firm called Benzole. I had always thought the name was made up purely for the sake of a schoolboy joke. 'She was only a garage man's daughter, but she loved the smell of Benzole.' Benzole was big oil firm, with plush offices in Newcastle. I went for the interview - and was turned down flat.

Apart from editing Palatinate in that last year at Durham, I was also elected Senior Man. It meant I was President of the Junior Common Room of my College, a position I was very proud of, and still am, though Margaret mocked the title all the time. And still does.

In Carlisle, during the summer of 1958, there was great excitement for the arrival of the Queen to celebrate Carlisle's Octocentenary. It was 800 years since Carlisle's first Royal Charter granted by Henry II in 1158 and there had been scores of special events going on all year.

I don't remember much about Carlisle's other big historic event of the 1950's, the Pageant of 1951. Presumably the Creighton School took part as most secondary schools provided the crowd scenes.

129

OCTOPIE

Copies of Octopie are now collector's items.

Margaret was in the second year at the High School and she wore a yellow smock top and rust coloured long shorts. She remembers them as being very rough and itchy. Cheap cloth was bought in bulk and mothers were given a cut-out pattern and made the appropriate costume for their child.

Annabelle and Marion, my sisters, then at the Margaret Sewell, wore bright red hessian dresses with a white collar. They were supposed to be peasant girls at the time of Mary Queen of Scots. They had a rehearsal in Bitts Park where they had to run after a posh lady on a horse. Marion didn't turn up for the Pageant itself, saying the whole thing was stupid, but Annabelle did, being law abiding.

For the 1958 celebrations, I had a small but very enjoyable role. I was asked to edit Octopie, a student magazine, a bit like a rag mag, with all proceeds going to charity, which was to be produced by Carlisle students as their contribution to the Octocentenary celebrations.

I wrote to the Art College, the Tech College, the sixth forms at the Grammar and High School, and all the Carlisle people I knew currently at university, asking for contributions. I got some good illustrations from the Art College, one of which I put on the cover, but most of the stuff I wrote myself, as very little came in, most of it useless, though Mary Hale, who had been head girl of the High School and gone to London University, did a very good piece in Cumbrian dialect.

I amused myself by doing a parody of the Cumberland News calling it the Cumberland Spews. I did a mock-up of its front page, making up silly news stories, getting my own back on them for not offering me a job. I included joke classified adverts, on the lines of many you saw in Cumbrian papers at the time.

The Cumberland News at the time always had lots of vacancies for 'Strong Lad Wanted' or 'Experienced lad', so naturally I turned it into 'Strong Lad Wanted For Strong Lass' or 'Experienced Lad wanted For Experienced Lass'. Another one said 'Cowman wanted at Candlemas - bring own cow and candle'. Well, it amused us at the time.

On the joke front page, under the banner 'Cumberland Spews' -

Cumberland
Spews

Incorporating "Stanwix Stench,"
"Botcherby Bilge" and
"The Dalston Dregs."

" BEST YEAR FOR OCTO-CENTENARY " – says Council

After a 16 hour long meeting of the Carlisle City Council last Tuesday, it was decided by five votes to four with twelve abstentions, that 1958 was after all the most appropriate year to hold the Octo-centenary celebrations.

Socialist members of the Council maintained that as 1158 was the year in which Carlisle had won the F.A. Jousting Competition and Henry II had given the city a Charter (Tom Beckett had disappeared with the cup again) it was obviously time for an Octo-centenary.

COUNCIL MUGS

But Conservative members said that 1158 and all that had nothing to do with it. The Socialists just wanted it this year as Ald. Smith had 4,000 coronation mugs left over from the Coronation he wanted to sell to the school children. " What was wrong with 1973 anyway," shouted Mr. J. J. J. Jones.

MORE BILGE

Councillor Bilge, Chairman of the Ways and Means Committee said: " I don't know what to do." Then as an afterthought, " Surely it's more than 100 years since Octo died ? "

Mr. Brown asked: " What about the Education Committee?" (Conservative cries of

year's holiday as part of the celebrations. Mr. Fitzriley (Caldewgate), a Conservative Councillor and Chairman of the Sewage Committee, thought it was " a bit off." Mr. Dilly proved that between 1945 and 1951, 1,676 council houses were built in Carlisle, an average of 449½ (loud cheers) and one washouse. The Mayor giggled and said his chain was tickling. Mr. Black said he shouldn't put it inside his shirt.

HIT RATEPAYERS

Finally it was agreed that 1958 was the best year and the one most likely to go far. The council was prepared to lash out even if it meant hitting the ratepayers. The Town Hall is to have a new flag, Citadel Square is going to be dug up and daffodils planted to read " floreat narcissus "; the workmen playing on the top of the station roof are to be given a day's holiday and Dr. Green is to compose a fantasia entitled " Hail to The Blithe

132

incorporating Stanwix Stench, Botcherby Bilge and Dalston Dregs, I had a joke advert for 'Jaspers - Slip Between Sheets, The Bawdy House, Carlisle'. Meaningless today, unless you remember Jespers of the Border House was a very select clothes shop and that students in the 1950's used to sing a song about 'Oh Sir Jasper do not touch me'.

Copies of Octopie are now collector's items, at least that's what I like to maintain. I have rarely ever seen them in secondhand shops which means, obviously, they are still being kept and treasured to this very day.

The Queen's visit, the culmination of the octo celebrations, and the focal point of six months of preparations, was timed for July 11, 1958. On the very morning she was due, the Duke of Edinburgh, who had already arrived, announced from the Town Hall that the Queen had been taken ill and gone straight on to London. You could hear the groans and Oh's from the thousands of people who had already gathered in the streets of Carlisle.

The Queen did return, some time later, but it wasn't quite the same. I didn't see her, as I wasn't in Carlisle by then. I had been accepted by both the newspaper training schemes I had applied for and had chosen the Kemsley one.

My first job in life, as opposed to the temporary ones I had done in Carlisle, was to be in Manchester, working on the Manchester Evening Chronicle.

I still treasure the letter sent to me by the news editor of the paper in August, 1958, Bob Walker, confirming my appointment and saying I would be on a salary of £14 a week. It seemed an enormous amount. When I showed the letter to my father, he said it was more than he'd ever got in the whole of his working life at 14 MU.

My mother was pleased, but apprehensive, thinking journalism was not a proper job, with no security, but at least I would have teaching to fall back on.

And so in the autumn of 1958 I cleared up my few things from my half of our bedroom in Caird Avenue and left Carlisle.

Chapter Fourteen

A Funeral and a Wedding

I started work on the Manchester Evening Chronicle on September 1, 1958. Its offices were in Withy Grove and the building was the biggest newsaper printing plant in Europe, perhaps the world. Over 10 million copies a week of up to twelve different papers were produced there. They included all the Northern editions of the national papers owned by Kemsley which a year later, in 1959, became Thomson Newspapers - such as The Sunday Times, Empire News, Sunday Graphic, Daily Sketch, Sporting Chronicle. They also produced the Northern editions of the Daily Telegraph, Daily Mirror, Sunday Mirror. Over 4,000 people worked in the building. Night and day, it never slept. The Evening Chronicle itself, so it said on the paper's mast head, had one million readers every evening.

I was overwhelmed by the building and by Manchester itself, compared with Carlisle, which wasn't surprising, as, at the age of 22, I had not been further south than Penrith. A slight exaggeration, though one I frequently came out with. I had been to France with the Creighton, and to London for the day for my Kemsley interview, but in essence it was true.

One of the minor things I had to get used to in Manchester was their use of the words 'North West'. When I first saw it as a headline in the Chron, on the lines of 'Family from North West lost in Spain' or 'North West Couple wins Pools' I thought oh, that's interesting, they've got a story about someone from Cumberland, perhaps from Carlisle, but of course it never was. We in Cumbria consider the North West as meaning Cumbria, where we live, which is clear enough to any fool looking at the map of England, but to media folks based in Manchester, the North West stretched in their minds from about Stoke to Scotland.

I had never been to Manchester before, didn't know one district from another, so from a map of Manchester I picked a flat as near as I could to the office, in order to get to work quickly. It was in Cheetham Hill which turned out a real dump, full of run down rain-coat factories. I called it a flat, but it was just a room on the ground floor at the front of an old terrace house with a kitchen in an alcove. I shared a bathroom with the other people in the house.

Margaret stayed with me there, when she came to visit, but of course I had to keep this secret from the landlord. I had taken it as a single man. If I had said it was for two, I would have to have proved I was married. Even in a run down area, landlords wouldn't let places to unmarried people in the 1950's.

One day, when we were in bed together, we thought we heard the landlord arriving for his rent. I jumped out while Margaret hid in the wardrobe. I stood in front of the bed, hoping to hide any signs of her presence, and handed over the rent to the landlord. As I did so, the bed, which was just a battered let-you-down couch, decided to put itself up, jack knifing together, giving Margaret a terrible fright, still hiding in the wardrobe.

Another time, we heard someone opening our bedroom window in the middle of the night and climbing into our room. I shouted out, scared stiff, and a voice in broken Polish, slightly the worse for drink, apologised and said he'd got the wrong house. He then climbed out again. He was obviously one of the workers from the sweated labour raincoat factory next door, so I turned over and went back to sleep. But Margaret didn't. Next day, she said how useless and feckless I had been in what could have been a nasty incident.

The Evening Chron was in deadly rivalry with the Evening

News which was owned by the Guardian. I used to meet some of their reporters on jobs and one day, covering some story at Manchester University, I met Harry Evans, the journalist who had been at the same Durham college as me, a few years earlier. He was now personal assistant to the editor of the Evening News.

He came for supper one evening in my so called flat, with his wife Enid, also from Durham. Margaret was staying with me at the time, otherwise I would never have attempted any sort of entertaining, and she made the room as attractive as possible, with candles and soft lights. She cooked fresh herring coated in oatmeal, very 1950's. Harry took one look at the fish and became worried about getting bones in his mouth. Suddenly he jumped up and switched on all the lights, and revealed the full horrors of the room.

Harry was never really interested in food anyway. Many years later, when he was editor of The Sunday Times and I was just leaving the editorship of the Colour Mag, he and Tina Brown, about to be his new wife, took Margaret and me to the Ivy Restaurant in London. I went through the menu, being a trencherman, while all Harry had that evening was a brussels sprouts omelette. Ugh.

When Margaret came to stay with me for longer periods, such as the summer vac, she couldn't of course tell her parents where she was and what she was doing, even though she was by then aged twenty and we had been going out together for about three years. Some of her well-off girl friends from Oxford were spending their summer in exotic places all over Europe, such as Venice, Florence, Rome. Margaret told her parents she had been invited to go along with one of them, staying at their family holiday home in Italy. Before they departed, Margaret wrote a series of letters to her parents from each of these places, with different dates, describing the different places, and the girl friends duly posted them to Carlisle on the correct dates. Margaret meanwhile was in a sunny Cheetham Hill with me.

Sounds daft now, and very complicated, but it worked and kept her mother happy. It has always made me wonder, when writing biographies of famous people, if letters supposedly written at a certain time from a certain place were in fact true or perhaps a cover for something we will never know about.

At Christmas time, 1958, I went home to Carlisle, as Margaret did, to stay with our respective parents. I slept with my brother Johnny in our shared bed, as I had always done when I lived at home.

On one occasion, on returning unexpectedly home from Durham, I found someone else in my bed. My mother had let out my half of the bed to a boy from a local home in Carlisle, Tony McMinn. He had just started his first job, on leaving the children's home, and needed digs. My mother had taken pity on him, and was also making a few bob for herself. He was a nice bloke, and later became a long distance lorry driver and often visited my mother with his own children, when he was in Carlisle.

My mother also had a long sequence of French assistants, male and female, who had secured teaching jobs at the Grammar School. Through Mr Watson, the head of French at the Grammar, they came to live with my mother for up to a year at a time. They all seemed to be called either Michel or Michelle. What was strange about these French teachers, at least to me at the time, is that they absolutely adored Carlisle, finding it exciting and exotic, even living in our council house in Caird Avenue. Years later, they often returned to Carlisle for their holidays, with their own families. We are still in touch with two of them, even now.

During my stay in Carlisle in the Christmas of 1958, I could see my father was very ill. He was still in the front parlour, bed-ridden through his multiple sclerosis, but he had now developed a very bad cold. On the night of December 27, just after all the Christmas festivities, I could hear my mother coming quietly into my bedroom. She said shush, don't move, don't get up, and she went to a chest of drawers and got out a clean white sheet.

I turned over and went to sleep, but subconsciously I knew what that must mean. When I got up in the morning, my father had died. On his death certificate, the official cause of death was pneumonia.

As the oldest child, and fortunately being at home at the time, I did all the official business, going to register his death and the assorted paper work. Reeves of Stanwix did his funeral but we had the funeral tea at our house, in Caird Avenue, to which all his Scottish relations came, as well as Margaret who helped my sisters to make the funeral tea. It was miserable weather, and a miserable occasion, right in the middle of that dead time of the year, between Christmas and the New Year.

He was buried in Carlisle Cemetery, up at the top, past all the graves of the war time servicemen. He was aged only 53 On his gravestone, his age is given as 52, but this is a mistake, my mother never being reliable on dates.

It seemed quite old to me at the time, being aged 52, but now I realise how young he was, cut off by illness, well before his prime. I have been counting every year since I turned 53 as a bonus.

He knew Margaret quite well by then, but he never saw us married. This happened on June 11, 1960, in Oxford Register Office, the day after Margaret's final exam at Oxford.

We didn't have a proper wedding, with guests and a reception, which rather disappointed my mother and Margaret's mother. We just couldn't face it, wanting to keep it private and quiet. It wasn't such a huge surprise to them, as we had been going out for so long. Mike Thornhill, my Carlisle friend still then at Balliol, and Margaret's college friend Theo, were our only witnesses.

I had bought my first car, a 1947 Riley for £100, which looked brilliant and classy but drove me mad as it was always going wrong. The day before our wedding, I failed my driving test, for the second time. Mike had to come in the car with us on the first stage of our honeymoon.

We were heading for London where we had secured a flat in the Vale of Health, right in the middle of Hampstead Heath. The year 1960 was not just the year I got married but the year I joined The Sunday Times.

So that was the 1950's over for me. And in effect the end of my Carlisle life.

End Bit

I said at the beginning I was happy to leave Carlisle, which had always seemed dull and dreary and boring when I lived there and appeared to offer nothing that I wanted out of life. It was true in the sense that Carlisle was not as attractive as it is today with very few of the wonderful facilities on offer now. The town centre was smoky, grey and industrial and our estate, St Ann's Hill, was grimy and dusty. But having looked back, trying to remember all the things that happened to me there - no doubt getting a few dates wrong, people and places incorrectly situated - I realise now that its appearance didn't really matter. It's what I did while I was there. Almost all of the vital things in my life did happen to me in Carlisle. As with the lives of most people, what you do up to the age of 21 can affect the rest of your life. In my case, it included going to the Grammar School, doing that little job on the Carlisle Journal, meeting Margaret.

As for the look and character of Carlisle, it began to change not long after I left. And by moving away, seeing other places, while observing how Carlisle was altering and improving, I began to appreciate more all the virtues and features of Carlisle. You often have to leave, in order to know where you are from.

Growing up in Carlisle in the 1950's, thinking I was in a vacuum, I imagined that the thoughts and experiences I and my friends were going through at the time were peculiar to Carlisle. It was only years later, interviewing people like the Beatles, on their childhood and school days in Liverpool, that I began to realise we were not alone. Not just riding the same Raleigh Lenton bike as John Lennon, loving all the Just William books, listening to the same music, wanting our trousers narrowed by neighbours, but so many of the emotions and feelings I had had were being shared by people of that age, at that time, all over Britain. Only the names of streets and shops and schools were different.

It wasn't just a class thing either. Later, when I got to know people of my age who had been to schools like Eton and Winchester, they too had loved Dick Barton and longed for the same sort of bike and tight trousers and had a Silloth in their life, for of course very few people in those days ever went abroad. I also now know that all towns have a Stanwix as well as a Raffles.

There was also the residue of the war, and the post war years of austerity. Rationing continued, which affected everyone living in Britain at that time, of whatever class, whatever region. The 1950's was a pretty grey period generally, now I look back in my mind's eye. There wasn't a lot of colour or richness of texture, in the nation's food, the clothes or the leisure lives of most people. Carlisle, in that sense, was not much different from other places.

But Carlisle was where the 1950's happened to happen to me. And for that, I will always be grateful.